how2become

How to join the Royal Air Force

Richard McMunn

Orders: Please contact How2become Ltd, Suite 3, 50 Churchill Square Business Centre, Kings Hill, Kent ME19 4YU. You can also order via the e-mail address info@how2become.co.uk.

ISBN: 9781907558580

First edition published 2010

Second edition published 2014

CONTENTS

WELCOME

Welcome to 'How 2 Become: The insider's guide to joining the RAF'. This guide has been designed to help you prepare for, and pass the Royal Air Force selection process relevant for Airmen/Airwomen and RAF Regiment Gunners.

The author of this guide, Richard McMunn, has spent over 20 years in both the Armed Forces and the Emergency Services. He has vast experience and knowledge in the area of Armed Forces recruitment and you will find his guidance both inspiring and highly informative. During his highly successful career in the Fire Service, Richard has sat on many interview panels, assessing a candidate's ability to obtain the job. He has also been extremely successful at passing job interviews himself and has a success rate of over 90%. Follow his advice and preparation techniques carefully and you too can achieve the same levels of success in your career.

Whilst the selection process for joining the Royal Air Force is highly competitive there are a number of things you can do in order to improve your chances of success, and they are all contained within this guide.

The guide itself has been split up into useful sections to make it easier for you to prepare for each stage. Read each section carefully and take notes as you progress. Don't ever give up on your dreams; if you really want to join the RAF then you can do it. The way to prepare for a job in the Armed Forces is to embark on a programme of 'in depth' preparation, and this guide will show you exactly how to do that.

If you need any further help with the RAF aptitude tests, getting fit or RAF interview advice, then we offer a wide range of products to assist you. These are all available through our online shop www.how2become.com. Once again, thank you for your custom, and we wish you every success in your pursuit of joining the Royal Air Force.

Work hard, stay focused and be what you want…

Best wishes,

The how2become team

The How2become Team.

PREFACE BY AUTHOR RICHARD MCMUNN

I can remember sitting in the Armed Forces careers office in Preston, Lancashire at the age of 16 waiting patiently to see the Warrant Officer who would interview me as part of my application for joining the Royal Navy. I had already passed the written tests, and despite never having sat an interview before in my life, I was confident of success.

In the build up to the interview I had worked very hard studying the job that I was applying for, and also working hard on my interview technique. At the end of the interview I was told that I had easily passed and all that was left to complete was the medical. Unfortunately I was overweight at the time and I was worried that I might fail. At the medical my fears became a reality and I was told by the doctor that I would have to lose a stone in weight before they would accept me. I walked out of the doctor's surgery and began to walk to the bus stop that would take me back home three miles away. I was absolutely gutted, and embarrassed, that I had failed at the final hurdle, all because I was overweight!

I sat at the bus stop feeling sorry for myself and wondering what job I was going to apply for next. My dream of joining the Armed Forces was over and I didn't know which way to turn. Suddenly, I began to feel a sense of determination to lose the weight and get fit in the shortest time possible. It was at that particular point in my life when things would change forever. As the bus approached I remember thinking there was no time like the present for getting started on my fitness regime. I therefore opted to walk the three miles home instead of being lazy and getting the bus. When I got home I sat in my room and wrote out a 'plan of action' that would dictate how I was going to lose the weight required. The plan of action was very simple and contained the following three rules:

1. Every weekday morning I will get up at 6am and run 3 miles.
2. Instead of catching the bus to college and then back home again I will walk.
3. I will eat healthily and I will not go over the recommended daily calorific intake.

Every day I would read my simple 'action plan' and it acted as a reminder of what I needed to do. Within a few weeks of following my plan rigidly I had lost over a stone in weight and I was a lot fitter too!

When I returned back to the doctor's surgery for my medical the doctor was amazed that I had managed to lose the weight in such a short space of time and he was pleased that I had been so determined to pass the medical. Six months later I started my basic training course with the Royal Navy.

Ever since then I have always made sure that I prepare properly for any job application. If I do fail a particular interview or section of an application process then I will always go out of my way to ask for feedback so that I can improve for next time. I also still use an 'action plan' in just about every element of my work today. Action plans allow you to focus your mind on what you want to achieve and I will be teaching you how to use them to great effect during this guide.

Throughout my career I have always been successful. It's not because I am better than the next person, but simply because I prepare better. I didn't do very well at school so I have to work a lot harder to pass the exams and written tests that form part of a job application process but I am always aware of what I need to do and what I must improve on.

I have always been a great believer in preparation. Preparation was my key to success, and it also yours. Without the right level of preparation you will be setting out on the route to failure. The RAF is hard to join, but if you follow the steps that I have compiled within this guide and use them as part of your preparation then you will increase your chances of success dramatically.

The men and women of the Armed Forces carry out an amazing job. They are there to protect us and our country and they do that job with great pride, passion and very high levels of professionalism and commitment. They are to be congratulated for the job that they do. Before you apply to join the RAF you need to be fully confident that you too are capable of providing that same level of commitment. If you think you can do it, and you can rise to the challenge, then you just might be the type of person the RAF is looking for.

CHAPTER ONE

INTRODUCTION

A career with the Royal Air Force is one of the best you can get within the British Armed Forces. The reason for this is that the technical expertise required to perform a large number of roles far exceeds some of the other roles within the Armed Forces. The application process, therefore, is considerably harder in terms of the technical knowledge that is required; if you are to achieve a pass and obtain the career that you are after.

Some of the roles and careers within the Royal Air Force require you to possess GCSEs in Maths, English and a science-based subject. However, there are a number of career options open to those who have no qualifications at all. Whichever career path you choose you will need to pass the initial selection process, which includes a number of tests and interviews. In order to progress through each stage of the selection process you must prepare fully and put in 100% effort. The emphasis throughout this guide is on preparation and this will be mentioned on a number of occasions. The majority of people who fail the Royal Air Force selection process do so through lack of preparation and not through an inability to achieve their goal. During your preparation it is important to remember that the smallest things can make the biggest difference. Try to imagine yourself as a Royal Air Force careers officer. What would you be looking for in potential applicants? A smart appearance, clean shoes, confidence, intelligence, manners and politeness perhaps? An ability to listen to what you are being told is also very important and if you are asked to attend an interview or test at a specific time and place then make sure you are there on time and do not be late.

During my time in the Armed Forces I had many amazing experiences and I met some fantastic people. By the time I was 19 I had travelled the world and seen places that others can only dream of – all whilst getting paid for it. Good things in life don't always come easy and you have to work very hard in order to achieve them. As I coach you through the selection process with the aid of this guide I want you to promise yourself one thing – that you will work hard and that you will always look for ways to improve on your weak areas.

During my time in the Armed Forces and Emergency Services I enjoyed a very successful career, despite leaving school with very few qualifications! My recipe for success has always been to work hard and improve myself. Perseverance and determination are favourite words of mine and if you apply them to your thinking whilst going through selection, and everything else that you do, then there is no reason why you can't achieve anything you want in life.

HOW TO PREPARE FOR THE RAF SELECTION PROCESS

Before I go into the different stages of the RAF selection process it is important for me to explain how you need to go about your preparation. Preparation is the process of getting yourself ready for the different stages of the selection process. In basic terms, the more preparation you do, your chances of success will increase. Do little or no preparation, then there is a high possibility that you will fail. It is also important to make a conscious effort to add some form of 'structure' to your preparation. For example, if I want to achieve something in life then I will always use an action plan. The action plan sets out what I am going to do and more importantly when I am going to do it. It's very similar to a shopping list in the fact that you are writing down exactly what you need to get or do whilst you are out shopping. Just by writing down the steps you are going to take in order to prepare for RAF selection you will be adding an element of 'structure' and 'organisation' to your work.

The following table is an action plan that I would use if I was going through selection right now.

MY ACTION PLAN FOR PREPARING FOR RAF SELECTION – EXAMPLE ONLY

Monday	Tuesday	Wednesday	Thursday	Friday	Saturday	Sunday
60 minutes Airman/ Airwoman Test preparation and 30 minutes reading about RAF history	60 minutes study relating to my choice of career	60 minutes Airman/ Airwoman Test preparation and 30 minutes reading about RAF history	Rest day	60 minute study relating to RAF life, airbases and equipment including my recruitment literature	60 minutes Airman/ Airwoman Test preparation and 30 minutes reading about RAF history	60 minutes study relating to my choice of career in the RAF
30 minute run then I will work on my sit ups and press ups	45 minutes gym work (light weights) including sit ups and press ups	30 minute run or bleep test preparation		1.5 mile run (best effort) and bleep test preparation. Also include some sit ups and press up work	45 minutes gym work (light weights) or 30 minute swim	60 minute study relating to RAF life, airbases and equipment including my recruitment literature

The above action plan/timetable would ensure that I focused on the following three key development areas:

1. Improving my mental and physical fitness in preparation for the selection process and in particular the pre-joining fitness test;
2. Improving my ability to carry out psychometric tests which will help me to pass the Airman/Airwoman Selection Test (AST);
3. Improving my knowledge of the RAF and my chosen career.

Of course, you will also need to work on your interview technique and responses to the questions but I will come onto that area in a later section of this guide. The point I am trying to get across here is that if you have some form of structure to your preparation then you are far more likely to succeed. By following a structured training and development programme during your preparation then you are far more likely to pass the RAF selection process. For every element of the RAF selection process use an action plan which sets out exactly what you are going to do, and when.

Lets now take a look at the different stages of the selection process for Airmen/Airwomen and RAF Regiment Gunners.

THE RAF SELECTION PROCESS RELEVANT FOR AIRMEN/ AIRWOMEN AND RAF REGIMENT GUNNERS

The selection process consists of the following stages:

Application form and initial interview at the Armed Forces Careers Office

↓

The Airman/Airwoman Selection Test (AST)

↓

Occupational Health Assessment

↓

The Pre-Joining Fitness Test

↓

Selection interviews and further checks

Once you have successfully passed every stage of the selection process then you will be offered a contract with the RAF. Once this is signed then you will receive a starting date for your initial basic training course. Let's now take a look at each of the different stages of selection.

APPLICATION FORM AND INITIAL INTERVIEW AT THE ARMED FORCES CAREERS OFFICE

The first stage of the RAF selection process is to submit your application. However, before you get to this stage it is important to speak to an Armed Forces Careers advisor about the options that are available to you and also about life within the RAF. You can find details of your nearest Armed Forces Careers Office by visiting the Royal Air Force website www.raf.mod.uk. On the website you will also find plenty of information about life in the RAF and the careers that are available. You should also discuss your choice of career with your family and with your partner to ensure that they give you their full support.

Once you have decided that a career in the RAF is for you then it is time to make your application. Remember, you are at no obligation to join until you sign your contract. There are two ways in which you can apply. The first and most efficient method is to apply online at the website www.raf.mod.uk. The second option is to complete the application form at your Armed Forces Careers Office. You will need to first of all register your details with the RAF before commencing your online application which usually takes approximately 45 minutes to complete. There are a number of different sections that you must complete including personal details, any experiences you have of the Armed Forces, details relating to your qualifications and finally information about your choice of career within the RAF. The application form is relatively simple to complete, however, there are a number of questions where you will need to provide evidence of your suitability for joining. For example, there will be questions that relate to your physical fitness and your involvement in sports and other similar activities. There will also be the opportunity to tell the RAF about any positions of responsibility you currently hold either at school, at home or at work. Whilst most of these questions are optional I would advise that you provide some brief details about any responsibilities you have held, or that you currently hold, as this will assist you in your application.

Examples of responsibilities an applicant may hold are as follows:

Responsibilities at school

'Whilst at school I was head of my class for the final year. During this time I was required to set an example to other pupils and inform the teacher of any missing pupils at the commencement of each lesson. I was also captain of the school hockey team for a period of time. Part of my responsibilities as captain included assisting teachers with the annual fixtures list and picking players for the team.

Responsibilities at work

'In my current job as sales assistant at a local retail store I am responsible for monitoring stock levels and ordering replenishments as and when required. I am also responsible for dealing with customer's enquiries and complaints as and when they arise.'

Responsibilities at home

'At home I am responsible for helping out with the cleaning. Part of my household responsibilities include cleaning the car and gardening on a weekly basis.'

If you have little or no responsibilities at present then it is certainly worth starting. You can add elements of responsibility to your life simply by carrying out household tasks such as cleaning, ironing or gardening. During your initial training course with the RAF you will be allocated certain responsibilities so it is advisable that you have some experience of responsibility before you join.

Once you have completed your application and it is successful you will then be invited to the Armed Forces Careers Office for an interview and to sit the Airman/Airwoman Selection Test (AST).

ARMED FORCES CAREERS OFFICE INTERVIEW

The initial interview will usually take place at the Armed Forces Careers Office and it is designed to assess your reasons for wanting to join the RAF, and your choice of career. If you have a Curriculum Vitae (CV) then I would suggest you take this along with you. If you do not already have a CV then you will find some useful tips on how to create one during a later section of the guide. The interview at the AFCO is sometimes referred to as a 'filter' interview and is designed to filter out those candidates who are suitable, and those who are not. During a later section of this guide I have provided a comprehensive section that will assist you in your preparation for the RAF interview.

Here are some useful tips that will help you to prepare:

- In the build up to the interview study the questions that are contained within this guide. Try to think of suitable responses for each question that are applicable to you and your circumstances.
- Make sure you already have some element of responsibility in your life either at home, at school or at work. Those candidates who can demonstrate experience of responsibility will score higher.
- Before you attend the interview visit the RAF's website

at www.raf.mod.uk and take a look at the career options that are available. Think very carefully about the type(s) of career that interests you. Think about the qualifications you have and any experiences you already have that might be suitable to your chosen career(s). During the interview the RAF will want to know what careers you are most interested in, and more importantly the reasons why.

- During the interview the RAF will ask you questions about any jobs you have had to date. If you have no experience of work then consider applying for a part time job either at weekends or in the evening. If you are finding it difficult to get part time work then even consider a few hours voluntary work. Providing evidence of previous work commitments during the interview will be a positive thing.
- During the interview there will be questions that relate to any hobbies you have and also your free time activities. Those candidates who can demonstrate that they use their leisure time actively will score higher. The RAF interviewer will want to see that you are an active person, as opposed to someone who sits at home on the computer for hours on end.
- The interviewer will want to know why you have chosen the RAF and not the other forces. They will also want to know what you've done to find out about the RAF and also your chosen career(s). Information about the RAF and your chosen career is very easy to find on the RAF's website www.raf.mod.uk. Make sure you learn as much as possible about the RAF, your chosen career(s) and in particular the training that you'll be required to undertake.

- Before you attend the interview read the assessable qualities that I have provided you within this guide. These will be a good basis for your preparation.
- When you attend the interview dress smartly. One of the most effective ways to create a good impression is by wearing a smart, formal outfit. Remember though, you can still look scruffy in a suit so make sure it is clean and pressed.
- Polish your shoes and have a good level of personal hygiene.
- Work on your interview technique and try out a mock interview before you attend the AFCO.

Once you have passed your interview then you will move on to the next stage of the selection process.

THE OCCUPATIONAL HEALTH ASSESSMENT AND PRE-JOINING FITNESS TEST

As part of the RAF selection process you will be required to undertake an Occupational Health Assessment and a Pre-Joining Fitness test. The RAF will be investing a large amount of time, money and resources into your training so they want to be sure that you are physically fit and healthy. The requirements for both the health assessment and the pre joining fitness test will vary for each role. Contact your AFCO advisor for more details. You will also find a useful guide entitled 'How to get RAF Fit' towards the end of this book which will assist you greatly during your preparation.

FURTHER SELECTION INTERVIEWS AND CHECKS

Some positions in the RAF will require further selection interviews and checks. The type of interview will vary depending on the role that you are applying for. Once again, check with your AFCO advisor to see if the job you are applying for qualifies for further interviews. Once you have successfully passed every stage of the selection process then you will be offered a contract of employment and you will receive a date for the commencement of your training.

CHAPTER TWO

HOW TO CREATE AN EFFECTIVE CV

As I discussed earlier in the guide it is advisable to take along with you to the careers office interview an accurate and up to date CV. During this section of the guide I will provide you with a step by step guide on how to create one.

The word Curriculum Vitae translated means the 'course of life'. CV's are used to demonstrate to an employer that you have the potential, the skills, and the experience to carry out the role you are applying for. Your CV is a very important document and you should spend sufficient time designing it so that it matches the job that you are applying as closely as possible.

WHAT MAKES AN EFFECTIVE CV?

In simple terms, an effective CV is one that matches the specification and the requirements of the job you are applying for. Your CV should be used as a tool to assist you during the initial stages of RAF selection and it should be centred on the following areas:

- Creating the right impression of yourself;
- Indicating that you possess the right qualities and attributes to perform the role of the job you are applying for;
- Grabbing the assessor's attention;
- Being concise and clear.

The most effective CV's are the ones that make the assessor's job easy. They are simple to read, to the point, relevant and focus on the job/role that you are applying for. CV's should not be overly long unless an employer specifically asks for this. Effective CV writing is an acquired skill that can be obtained relatively quickly with a little bit of time, effort and focus.

Before you begin to start work on your CV it is a good idea to have a basic idea of how a job/person specification is constructed. A job description/person specification is basically a blueprint for the role you are applying for; it sets out what the employer expects from potential applicants. One of your main focus points during the construction of your CV will be to match the job/person specification. Most job/person specifications will include the following areas:

EXPERIENCE REQUIRED: previous jobs, unpaid work experience, life experience, skills, knowledge and abilities: for example, languages, driving, knowledge of specialist fields, ability to use equipment, plus some indication of the level of competence required, and whether the person must have the skills or knowledge beforehand or can learn them on the job.

QUALIFICATIONS REQUIRED: exams, certificates, degrees, diplomas (some jobs require specific qualifications, but most do not and it can be fairer to ask for the skills or knowledge represented by the qualification rather than asking for the qualification itself).

PERSONAL ATTRIBUTES REQUIRED: such as strength, ability to lift, willingness to work in a hectic busy environment or on one's own.

PERSONAL CIRCUMSTANCES: such as being able to work weekends or evenings or even to travel.

Most job/person specifications will be based around a task analysis of the vacancy, so there should be nothing within the job description/person specification that is irrelevant or that does not concern the particular role you are applying for. Whatever requirements you are asked to meet, you should try hard to match them as closely as possible, providing evidence if possible of your previous experience.

WHAT IS THE AFCO RECRUITMENT ADVISOR LOOKING FOR IN YOUR CV?

As previously stated you should ensure that you make the recruitment advisor's job as simple as possible. Try to put yourself in the shoes of the assessor. How would you want an applicants CV to look? You would want it to be relevant to role they are applying for and you would want it to be neat, concise and well organised.

For the majority of jobs in the RAF there will be job specification or person specification. You need to spend some time thinking about the type of person they are looking for and how you can match the specification that is relevant to the job you want. Most job specifications will list the essential/

desirable requirements in terms of education, qualifications, training, experience, skills, personality and any other special requirements.

Let's take a look at some of the skills and qualifications required to become a Physical Training Instructor in the RAF.

Qualifications required	About the job
You will need 2 GCSEs/SCEs or equivalent, in the subjects of English language at Grade C/3 minimum and in Mathematics at Grade G/6 minimum. You will need to have a good standard of fitness in a number of sports and have the ability to swim. You will be assessed via a specialist interview and be required to undertake additional tests.	Physical Training Instructors are responsible for organising and arranging physical fitness training programmes for all members of the RAF. Therefore a good standard of physical fitness and organisational skills are required. In addition to being physically fit you must also possess good motivational skills. • Manage and arrange adventure activities; • Manage sporting facilities; • Organise and conduct instructional classes; • Perform fitness tests; • Arrange and hold sports counselling sessions.

You will see from the above details that some of the key elements of the role include suitable levels of physical fitness, good organisational skills, motivational skills and the ability to manage people and resources. Once you have the above information then you will be able to mould your CV around the key aspects of the job.

Before I provide you with a sample CV that is based on matching the above role, let's first of all take a look at some of the key elements of a CV.

THE KEY ELEMENTS OF A CV

The following is a list of information I recommend you include within your CV. Try to put them in this order and remember to be brief and to the point. Make sure you include and highlight the positive aspects of your experience and achievements.

- Your personal details
- Your profile
- Your employment history
- Your academic acievements
- Your interests
- Any other information
- Your references

Let's now take a look at each of the above sections and what you need to include.

YOUR PERSONAL DETAILS

When completing this section you should include the following details:

- Your full name
- Address
- Date of birth
- Nationality
- Contact telephone numbers including home and mobile
- E-mail address

YOUR PROFILE

To begin with try to write a brief but to the point statement about yourself making sure you include the keywords that best describe your character. Some effective words to use when describing yourself might include:

Ambitious, enthusiastic, motivated, caring, trustworthy, meticulous, sense of humour, drive, character, determination, will to succeed, passionate, loyal, teamwork, hard working.

The above words are all powerful and positive aspects of an individual's character. Try to think of your own character and what positive words you can use that best describe you.

Within your profile description try to include a statement that is relative to you and that will make the assessor think you are the right person for the job, such as:

"I am an extremely fit and active person who has a great deal of experience in this field and I have a track record of high achievement. I have very good organisational and motivational skills and I am always striving to improve myself. I believe that I would embrace the challenges that this new role has to offer."

YOUR EMPLOYMENT HISTORY

When completing this section try to ensure that it is completed in reverse chronological order. Provide the reader with dates, locations and employers, and remember to include your job title. Give a brief description of your main achievements and try, again, to include words of a positive nature, such as:

Achieved, developed, progressed, managed, created, succeeded, devised, drove, expanded, directed.

It is also a good idea to quantify your main achievements, such as:

"During my time with this employer I was responsible for motivating my team and organising different activities."

YOUR ACADEMIC ACHIEVEMENTS

When completing this section include the dates, names and locations of the schools, colleges or universities that you attended in chronological order.

You should also include your qualifications and any other relevant achievements such as health and safety qualifications or first aid qualifications. Anything that is relevant to the role you're applying for would be an advantage.

YOUR INTERESTS

Within this section try to include interests that match the requirements of the job and ones that also portray you in a positive manner. Maybe you have worked within the voluntary sector or have even carried out some charity work in the past? If so try to include these in your CV as they show you have a caring and concerning nature. You may also play sports or keep fit, in which case you should include these too. If you have any evidence of where you have worked effectively as part of a team then include these also.

ANY OTHER INFORMATION

Within this section of your CV you can include any other information that is relevant to your skills or experiences that you may feel are of benefit. Examples of these could certificates of achievement from work or school.

REFERENCES

Although you will normally be required to provide two references as part of you application for joining the RAF, it is good practice to include these at the end of your CV. Try to include your current or previous employer, providing you know that they are going to write positive things about you. Be careful who you choose as a reference and make sure you seek their permission first prior to putting down their name and contact details. It may also be a good idea to ask them if you can have a copy of what they have written about you for reference later.

SAMPLE CV

The following sample CV has been designed to give you an idea of how an effective CV might look. It has been created with the position of Physical Training Instructor in mind. All of the information provided is fictitious.

Curriculum Vitae of Richard McMunn

Address: 75, Any Street, Anytown, Anyshire. ANY 123
Date of birth: 01/01/1970
Nationality: British
Telephone contact: 01227 XXXXX / Mobile 07890 XXX XXX
E-Mail contact: richardmcmunn@anyemailaddress.co.uk

Personal profile of Richard McMunn

I am an extremely fit and active person who has a great deal of experience in this field and I have a track record of high achievement. I have very good organisational and motivational skills and I am always striving to improve myself. I believe that I would embrace the challenges that this new role has to offer. I am a motivated, dedicated, loyal and ambitious person who has the ability to work both within a team and also unsupervised.

I already have a large amount of experience in the working environment and take on a large number of responsibilities both at work, around the home and in my leisure time activities. I am currently the Captain of my local football team and part of my responsibilities includes organising and conducting weekly evening training sessions for the team. For every training session that I run I always try to vary the type of exercises that we perform. This allows me to maintain everyone's motivation and interest levels. For example, one week I will organise the Multi Stage Fitness Test and another week we will practice tackling and dribbling skills.

To conclude, I am a fit, motivated active, organised and professional individual who has a lot of skills and experiences to offer the RAF.

Employment history of Richard McMunn (in chronological order)

Job position/title/company #1 goes here **Date of employment goes here**

During my time with this employer I was responsible for motivating my team and organising different activities.

Job position/title/company #2 goes here **Date of employment goes here**

During my time with this employer I was responsible stock taking and dealing with customer's queries and complaints. I also took on the responsibility of arranging the company's annual staff leisure activity event which often included some form of motivational talk.

Job position/title/company #3 goes here **Date of employment goes here**

During my time with this employer I undertook a training course in health and safety and first aid. Part of my role included managing resources and training rooms/equipment.

Academic achievements of Richard McMunn

Health and Safety qualification	**Date of achievement goes here**
First Aid qualification	**Date of achievement goes here**
Level 1 Physical Training Instructor qualification	**Date of achievement goes here**
GSCE Maths Grade C	**Date of achievement goes here**
GCSE English Grade C	**Date of achievement goes here**
GCSE Physical Education Grade B	**Date of achievement goes here**

Interests and Hobbies of Richard McMunn

I am an extremely fit and active person who carries out a structured training programme at my local gym five times a week. During my training sessions I will carry out a variety of different exercises such as indoor rowing, cycling, treadmill work and light weights. I measure my fitness levels by performing the multi-stage fitness test once a week and I can currently achieve level 14.5. In addition to my gym work I am a keen swimmer and break up my gym sessions with long swim sessions twice a week. I can swim 60 lengths of my local swimming pool in time of 35 minutes.

I am also the Captain of my local football team and play in the position of midfield. I am also responsible for organising and arranging the weekly training sessions.

In addition to my sporting activities I like to relax with a weekly Yoga group at my local community centre. I also have a keen interest in art and attend evening classes during the months October through to December.

Further information

Six months ago I decided to carry out a sponsored fitness event in order to raise money for a local charity. I swam 60 lengths of my local swimming pool, and then ran 26 miles before cycling 110 miles all in one day. In total I managed to raise over £10,000 for charity.

References

Name, address and contact details of reference #1

Name, address and contact details of reference #2

TOP TIPS FOR CREATING AN EFFECTIVE CV

New application = new CV

It is important that every time you apply for a job you re-evaluate the content of your CV so that you can match the skills and qualifications required. As a rule you should complete a new CV for every job application unless your applications are close together and the job/person specification is relatively the same. Don't become complacent or allow your CV to get out of date.

Don't pad out your CV

There is a common misconception amongst many job applicants that you need to make your CV scores of pages long for it to get recognised. This simply isn't true. When creating your CV aim for quality rather than quantity. If I was looking through an applicant's CV then I would much prefer to see three pages of high quality focused information rather than 30 pages padded out with irrelevance.

Create a positive image

Writing an effective CV involves a number of important aspects. One of those is the manner in which you present your CV. When developing your CV ask yourself the following questions:

- Is your spelling, grammar and punctuation correct?
- Is it legible and easy to read?
- Is the style in which you are writing your CV standardised?
- Is it neat?
- Is it constructed in a logical manner?

By following the above tips in respect of your CV image you will be on the right track to improving your chances of getting the job you are after. You should spend just as much time on the ***presentation*** of your CV as you do on the ***content***.

Do you have the right qualities and attributes for the job you are applying for?

When you are developing your CV have a look at the required personal qualities that are listed within the job/person spec. Try to match these as closely as possible but, again, ensure that you provide examples where appropriate. For example, in the sample job description for a Physical Training Instructor one of the required personal qualities was to:

'Organise and conduct instructional classes'

Try and provide an example of where you have achieved this in any previous roles. The following is a fictitious example of how this might be achieved:

"I am currently the Captain of my local football team and part of my responsibilities include organising and conducting weekly evening training sessions for the team. For every training session that I run I always try to vary the type of exercises that we perform. This allows me to maintain everyone's motivation and interest levels. For example, one week I will organise the Multi Stage Fitness Test for them and another week I will arrange practice tackling and dribbling skills."

Matching your qualities and attributes to the role you are applying for is very important.

Be honest when creating your CV

If you lie on your CV, especially when it comes to academic qualifications or experience, you will almost certainly get caught out at some point in the future. Maybe not straight away but even a few months or years down the line an employer can still dismiss you for incorrect information that you provide during the selection process. It simply isn't worth it. Be honest when creating your CV and if you don't have the right skills for the job you are applying for, then go out there and get them!

Now that I've shown you how to create an effective CV, schedule into your action plan a date and time when you intend to create your own. Now let's move on to my top 10 tips for success.

CHAPTER THREE

MY TOP 10 TIPS FOR SUCCESS

Over the next few pages I have provided you with a number of important tips that I believe will help you pass the RAF selection process. Many of the tips are simple ones; however, the majority of candidates I come across implement very few of them and they end up failing as a result. Follow each tip carefully and make sure you implement them into your preparation strategy and action plan.

TIP NUMBER 1 – PREPARE FULLY FOR EVERY STAGE OF THE SELECTION PROCESS

As I have already stated at the beginning of this guide, preparation is crucial to your success. Those people who prepare fully for selection will do well. If you don't prepare fully then there is a strong possibility that you will fail.

There are a number of important things that you can do in order to improve your chances of success. The first important area is your research of the RAF and the role(s) that you are applying for. During the selection interview(s) the RAF will want to see that you have studied their organisation, your choice of career and the training that you will undergo if you are successful. The only way to do this is to sit down and read your recruitment literature, study the RAF website at www.raf.mod.uk and to also speak to serving members of the RAF. You may also find it useful to learn a little bit about the history of the service. Whilst not essential, it will demonstrate to the assessors that you have gone out of your way to learn as much as possible about the organisation, its success stories, and what it stands for. When you come on to the interview section of this guide you will note that I have provided you with lots of sample questions and answers that will assist your during your preparation.

I also mentioned in an earlier section of the guide that I recommend you implement some form of action plan into your preparation. This will make sure that your preparation is focused and targeted on the right areas. For example, if you have never attended an interview before then it is wise that you carry out a 'mock interview' before you attend the real one. This involves getting a friend or member of your family to sit down and interview you using the questions that are contained within this guide. The more mock interviews that you do, the better you'll become.

It is also important to work on your ability to pass the Airman/Airwoman Selection Test, or AST as it is otherwise called. The AST consists of a number of different psychometric tests that are designed to assess your ability to carry out tasks quickly and accurately. Within a separate section of this guide I have provided you with lots of different test questions to help you prepare. I would recommend that you carry out lots of sample test questions over a prolonged period of time, as opposed to 'cramming' the night before. Little and often is the key to improvement and it is also important to check which answers you got wrong so that you can improve for next time.

TIP NUMBER 2 – PRACTICE PLENTY OF PSYCHOMETRIC TEST QUESTIONS

The RAF has made brilliant progress in its aptitude testing policies over the years and in particular the quality and the range of tests it uses. The tests that they use to assess potential candidates are now driven by detailed analyses of training requirements. This effectively means that if you score poorly on the tests then there is a strong likelihood that you will not be able to perform your role in the RAF competently.

During the selection process for joining the RAF you will be required to sit the Airman/Airwoman Selection Test. The test itself is multiple choice in nature and it covers seven specific areas. It is designed to assess your ability to carry out tasks quickly and accurately. Your results in the test will determine your suitability for a career in the RAF so it is very important that you achieve the highest scores possible. How you achieve that is through 'deliberate' and 'repetitive' practice. Deliberate and repetitive practice involves finding out which areas you need to improve on, and then carrying out lots of practice in that particular area, until you become competent.

The AST consists of:

- A verbal reasoning test which is designed to assess your ability to use and understand written information;
- A numerical reasoning test which assesses your ability to work with numbers and carry out mathematical

calculations such as fractions and formulae and also your ability to use different graphs and tables;

- A spatial reasoning test that will examine your understanding of how shapes and different objects rotate and move;
- A work rate test which will assess how quickly you can carry out specific tasks;
- An electrical comprehension which is used to assess your level of electrical competence;
- A memory test;
- A mechanical comprehension test. This test is used to examine how well you understand mechanical concepts.

As you progress through this guide you will notice that I have included lots of sample test questions that will help you to prepare for the different tests. You will need to set aside plenty of time in the build up to your AST in order to practise them. Use the questions within this book to help you prepare. Just by practising lots of similar test to the ones you'll be required to take at the AST your mind will begin to work faster under pressurised conditions. Whilst working through the tests make sure you check which questions you get wrong. This is a crucial part of your development.

If you feel that you still need assistance with the tests after carrying out lots of practice then I recommend you use a personal tutor.

TIP NUMBER 3 – BE POLITE AND COURTEOUS AND CREATE THE RIGHT IMPRESSION AT ALL TIMES

When you apply to join the Royal Air Force you will be communicating at times with experienced and professional serving RAF Officers and recruitment staff. They are highly trained to pick out those people who they believe are worthwhile investing time and money in, and they will be assessing you right from the word go. Whenever you make contact with the careers office, either by phone or in person, make sure you are polite, courteous and go out of your way to create the right impression. When I was going through the Armed Forces selection process I would always make an effort to dress smart when attending the careers office. There would always be other applicants at the office who were wearing jeans or tracksuits and trainers. Whilst there is no requirement to dress smart when you attend the careers office I believe it will go along way to helping you impress the recruitment staff.

When you telephone the careers office to either obtain an application form or arrange an informal chat then I advise that you are polite and courteous at all times. General good manners such as “good morning”, “good afternoon”, “thank you for your time” and “please” are not as commonplace in today’s society as they used to be. Being polite and courteous when you communicate with the careers officer can help you to create the right impression from the word go. Members of the Armed Forces, including those of the Royal Air Force, are role models in society. How would you expect a member of the RAF to behave? They would be smart, courteous and polite of course, and therefore, so should you. Even though you will not yet have joined the RAF, you should still demonstrate your potential at every opportunity. During my research into this guide I spoke to many serving officers. One in particular told me that she would be far more impressed if an applicant attended the careers office dressed smart, clean and tidy and with polished shoes. Unfortunately, she said, it doesn't happen that often.

TIP NUMBER 4 – BE SMART, CLEAN AND TAKE A PRIDE IN YOUR APPEARANCE

At the end of my initial Armed Forces basic training I received an award for being the best on my course for 'kit upkeep and bearing'. I'd worked very hard throughout my training and always ensured I looked smart and took a pride in my appearance. I can remember the Warrant Officer taking us for drill every Friday morning and he would shout out at the top of his voice – "Shiny shoes, shiny mind!" What a great statement I used to think. What he was essentially saying is that if you take a pride in your appearance then your mind will be more positive and you'll feel better about yourself. If you feel good about yourself then this will reflect in everything that you do.

How many people do you know clean their shoes every day? Not many, I'm sure, but this can go a long way to creating the right impression. Walking into the careers office with dirty shoes will not create a good impression and neither will dirty nails or generally poor personal hygiene. When you join the RAF you will be living and sleeping with lots of people in the same room. Approximately thirty people will give you some idea of how many you'll be living with. Therefore, personal hygiene is important and you will need to create an ability to look after yourself and your equipment. As an RAF recruit you will be inspected every day on your turnout, and it is far better to demonstrate to the careers officer that you have the ability to be smart before you begin your basic training. Your budget may not be big but you can purchase a shirt and tie for little money nowadays. They don't have to be expensive quality, but showing that you've made an effort will again create the right impression. If you cannot afford to buy a shirt and tie then you may be able to borrow these items from a friend or relative. It is definitely worth investing time and effort on your appearance as jeans, t-shirt and trainers are possibly not the best option. Treat every visit to the RAF Careers Office as an opportunity to impress.

Remember – you only get ONE chance to create a first impression!

TIP NUMBER 5 – GET FIT FOR THE PRE JOINING FITNESS TEST

Before you apply to join the Royal Air Force you may already be physically active and fit but, even so, it is essential that you make your life as easy as possible. During the selection process you will need to pass the Pre-Joining Fitness Test (PJFT) which, at the time of writing, consists of a 1.5 mile run in a time of 12 minutes and 12 seconds for men and 14 minutes and 35 seconds for women. The test will be carried out at either your local Armed Forces Careers Office or alternatively a gymnasium. The PJFT for joining the RAF Regiment however is tougher. For the RAF Regiment you will be required to undertake the Multi Stage Fitness Test, sit ups and press ups, a 3 mile run and a swimming test. The test is undertaken over three days at RAF Honnington in Suffolk. At the end of this guide I have provided you with a 'How to get RAF fit' guide, which has been designed to assist you in your preparation. The guide is suitable for candidates who are applying for both regular service and the RAF Regiment.

One of the most effective ways to improve your physical

fitness is to embark on a structured running programme. Just by running three miles, three times a week you will be amazed at how much your fitness and general well-being will improve. Being physically fit means you will be mentally fit too and your confidence will increase. Whatever the standard is during the selection process I advise that you aim to better it during your preparation.

When I was going through selection for the Armed Forces I forced myself to get up at 6am every weekday morning and go for a three mile run. It was tough, especially during the cold mornings, but I soon lost weight and got fit in the process. Getting up at 6am also prepares you for your basic training. After all, you won't be able to lie in bed all morning once your training starts!

Keep trying to improve yourself and remember – be the best that you can.

TIP NUMBER 6 – BE ABLE TO MATCH THE ASSESSABLE QUALITIES

During the RAF selection process you will be assessed against a number of different areas including:

- Your personal turnout and hygiene;
- How physically active and fit you are;
- How well you interact and mix with other people;
- Your ability to work as an effective team member;
- Your levels of maturity and professionalism;
- Your drive and determination to succeed;
- Being self reliant and responsible;
- How you react to discipline;

- Experience of and reaction to regimentation and routine;
- Your knowledge of the RAF;
- How motivated you are to join the RAF;
- Your personal circumstances.

The above areas will be assessed during your visits to the AFCO and also during the interviews. Some of the assessable areas are easier to demonstrate than others. For example, your knowledge of the RAF and your chosen career is easy to demonstrate, providing that is you put in the effort to learn the information. Being self reliant and responsible however is a different matter. In order to achieve this you will need to provide evidence of any responsibilities you have either at work, school or at home. If you have no responsibility whatsoever then now is the time to start. Just by taking on weekly household tasks such as cleaning or ironing you will demonstrating some form of responsibility at home. If you are currently employed then ask your manager if it is possible to take on extra responsibility. Having examples of where you have already met each of the assessable qualities will work in your favour. Within this guide I have provided a complete section that provides evidence on how you can match each of the above areas.

TIP NUMBER 7 – BE A COMPETENT TEAM PLAYER

During the selection process you will be assessed against your ability to work as an effective team player. Let's take a moment to write down some of the more prominent qualities that an effective team player should possess:

- An ability to interact and work with others, regardless of their age, sex, religion, sexual orientation, background, disability or appearance;

- Be able to communicate with everyone in the team and provide the appropriate level of support and encouragement;
- Be capable of carrying out tasks correctly, professionally and in accordance with guidelines and regulations;
- Being focused on the team's ultimate goal(s);
- Having a flexible attitude and approach to the task;
- Putting the needs of the team first before your own;
- Putting personal differences aside for the sake of the team;
- Being able to listen to others suggestions and contributions.

The Royal Air Force prides itself on its great ability to operate as an effective team. Try to think of the best football teams in the country. Those that are the most successful are not the ones that have one or two great players but the ones that have the best team overall. The ability to work as part of a team is essential and you will be assessed on this during the selection process. Within the Royal Air Force you will be required to work as a team every day in to carry out tasks both large and small. During the interview there is a strong possibility that you'll be asked questions that relate to your knowledge of how a team operates and also your experiences of working in a team to achieve a common task or goal. Before you move on to the next tip try to think of an occasion when you have worked effectively in a team to successfully achieve a goal or task. An example of this might be where you have played team sports or team activities.

TIP NUMBER 8 – PRACTICE A MOCK INTERVIEW BEFORE THE REAL THING

During the selection process you will be required to sit a number of interviews designed to test your suitability to join the RAF. In addition to the assessable qualities that I have already provided you will also be assessed on how well you present yourself during the interview. The RAF recruitment officers are looking for your potential and ability to become a professional and competent member of their team. They are not looking for the finished article but they certainly want to see potential. One of the most effective ways in which to prepare for the interview is to carry out a number of 'mock interviews' prior to the real thing. A mock interview is basically a practice run where you get a friend or relative to sit you down under formal interview conditions and ask you a series of questions. You simply respond to each interview question that is asked and make any necessary improvements at the end of the interview.

Why is it important to carry out a mock interview? Well, look at it this way, any team or professional individual will always practice their role or job before they do the real thing. An actor will rehearse his or her lines before filming, a football team will practise set pieces before a match and a professional swimmer will practise many lengths and improve their technique before the big race. Therefore, any serious candidate applying for a job will practise the interview before hand. Not only will it allow them to increase their confidence but it will also go a long way to reducing nerves and fear.

During the real RAF interview you need to create the right impression from the clothes that you wear to how you communicate, even down to how you sit in the interview chair. The interview is obviously an integral part of the selection process and within this guide I have provided a section dedicated solely to this. Look at the sample interview questions and prepare your responses beforehand by way of a mock interview. Don't go into your interview ill-prepared; instead, understand what is involved and what you need to do to impress the panel.

TIP NUMBER 9 – KEEP UP TO DATE WITH CURRENT AFFAIRS

In the build up to your selection interview I would recommend that you keep up to date with current affairs, especially in relation to whereabouts the RAF are operating at the time of your application. Try to watch the news and read newspaper articles, searching for information relating to any recent Armed Forces issues. These don't have to be specific to the Royal Air Force, but if you are joining a military organisation then it would be wise for you to be up to speed with current affairs. The type of newspaper that you read is important. Make sure you choose a quality newspaper that will provide you with accurate and up to date information. During the interview you may get asked a question along the following lines:

"Can you tell me whereabouts the Royal Air Force are operating in the world right now?"

The only way to know the answer to this question is by keeping up to date with current affairs and topical issues that are relevant to the RAF. I would also advise that you pick a few topical current affairs subjects, be aware of them, and also have an opinion of them. This will demonstrate to the recruitment staff that you are fully aware of current topical issues and that you can also form an opinion of them.

The following websites are useful tools for researching

information relevant to the UK Armed Forces and the Royal Air Force:

www.raf.mod.uk
www.mod.uk
www.rafnews.co.uk
www.rafcom.co.uk

Please note: How2become Ltd is not responsible for the content of any external websites.

TIP NUMBER 10 – GET SOME EXPERIENCE OF BEING SELF RELIANT

During the selection process the RAF recruitment staff will want to see some experience of where you have either been self reliant, or been away from you're home comforts for a period of time. The reason for this is simple; when you join the RAF you will embark on a nine week training course that will change your life forever. Not only will you be required to live with lots of other people in the same room but you will also be required to fend for yourself. Those people who have no experience of being self reliant or have never experienced 'communal living' will struggle. Of course, it's easy for anybody to say "I won't have any problems with leaving home or with being self reliant", but providing examples of where you have already experienced being self reliant is a different matter. Provide the interviewer or recruitment staff with examples of where you have been away from home for long periods such as camps, school trips or adventure trips. Tell them what activities you were involved in and also any responsibilities you had whilst being away from home.

If you have little or no experience so far of being self reliant then I recommend you get some! There are plenty of opportunities available to you such as going camping with friends for a weekend or you could even go away on an adventure trip or holiday. Whatever activity you decide to take part in, make sure it is safe.

BONUS TIP – LEARN THE VALUES OF THE RAF

Any organisation or service worth its salt will develop a set of values or standards that it expects its employees to abide by. The reason why an organisation will develop these standards is because it wants to deliver or provide a very high level of service.

During your research and study into the RAF I strongly recommend that you learn its values. When the recruitment officer at the Armed Forces Careers Office asks you 'what have you learnt about the RAF', you will be able to tell him or her that you have taken the time to learn these important values and also what they mean. They will be impressed that you have gone out of your way to learn them. The values of the RAF include:

- Having self **respect** and being respectful of others;
- Having **integrity** which means being responsible, honest and courageous;
- Having physical courage, loyalty, commitment and being able to work as part of a team during your **service**;
- Having personal **excellence**, being proud and self disciplined.

The most effective way to memorise the values is to simply remember the word 'RISE':

R = Respect

I = Integrity

S = service

E = Excellence

In addition to a set of values the RAF also has what is called an 'ethos' statement. This is basically a statement of how it intends to go about its business. The following is the RAF's ethos statement.

'Our distinctive character, spirit and attitude that is necessary to pull together as a team, in order to deliver air power no matter the challenges or environment. We place unit and Royal Air Force success above self and strive to be courageous in the face of adversity and risk. Sustained by strong leadership, high professional and personal standards, we are bound by a strong sense of tradition and belonging to an organization of which we are immensely proud.' (Crown Copyright ©)

Make sure you learn the ethos statement and the values of the RAF before you go to your interview.

CHAPTER FOUR

THE ASSESSABLE QUALITIES

In the previous section I provided you with an important tip that related to preparation. During this guide I am teaching you how to become the ideal candidate and part of that process involves having the ability to match each of the assessable qualities. In this section I will explain each of the different assessable qualities and what you can do to match them. Please note that the following list of qualities is not exhaustive and you may find that each recruitment officer will look for additional qualities and experiences depending on the role you are applying for.

PERSONAL TURNOUT AND HYGIENE

Whenever you attend the AFCO I advise that you attend in a smart outfit and that you also pay attention to your personal hygiene. In basic terms this means making sure you are well presented and that you've taken the time to wash! Before you go to the ACFO take a shower, wash your hair and clean your nails. The smallest things will make a difference and you will be demonstrating to the AFCO staff that you are capable of looking after yourself; something which is crucial to the role of an RAF Airman/Airwoman. Attend in jeans, trainers and with poor personal hygiene then this could work against you.

BE PHYSICALLY ACTIVE AND PHYSICALLY FIT

There are two elements here that need to be addressed. With the advent of the computer and electronic games more and more people, especially younger people, are spending longer hours on the computer. The average person now spends approximately 25 minutes everyday on the computer and that figure is set to rise as the year's progress. We are less active now as nation than we have ever been which only leads to one thing – a decrease in physical fitness levels. When you join the RAF you will be joining an organisation that requires its men and women to both physically active and physically fit. Therefore, the RAF recruitment staff will want to see evidence of these two important attributes during selection. They are very easy demonstrate. If you do little or no physical exercise at present then now is the time to change. At the end of this guide I have provided you with a fitness guide that contains a number of useful exercises that the majority of, can be carried out without the need to attend a gym. Embark on a structured training programme in the build up to selection and you will score higher in this area.

How well you interact and mix with other people and your ability to work as an effective team member

As I'm sure you've probably gathered already, being able to operate effectively as part of a team is important. Without an effective team the RAF wouldn't operate. That doesn't just mean the members of the RAF team who are fighter pilots; but also administrative workers and support staff who all play a very important part too. Even the office cleaners are just as important as the pilots when it comes to the effective operation of the team. The RAF requires its staff to be able to interact and mix with everyone else in the team, regardless of their background or their role. During the selection process they will want to see evidence of where you have already mixed with other people and where you have worked as part of a team in order to achieve a common goal or task. In the build up to selection try to think of occasions where you have already worked as part of a team and interacted with other people. A great example might be where you have played team sports or where you are a member of group or youth organisation.

YOUR LEVELS OF MATURITY AND PROFESSIONALISM

How mature are you as a person? Do you approach setbacks in life with optimism or do you sit back and complain, often feeling sorry for yourself? Everybody experiences some form of setback during their life but it is how you deal with it that is important. How did/do you approach your education? Did you work hard and give it your best? Do you carry out your job to the best of your ability? All of these things will provide the recruitment staff with an indication of how you are likely to perform as an Airman/Airwoman. Your training will be tough; however, if you go into it with a positive attitude and with a professional approach, then you are far more likely to succeed. Always look to continuously improve yourself in everything that you do.

YOUR DRIVE AND DETERMINATION TO SUCCEED

I am a driven person and I've always been enthusiastic. I've found that if I persevere and work hard then success will usually follow. If you have a history of success and you can demonstrate to the recruitment staff that you are determined to succeed then this will work in your favour. For example, if you find in the build up to the selection process that you are weak in a certain area, take positive steps to improve it. During the RAF interview you will be able to provide evidence to the recruitment staff of how determined you have been to improve. Here's an example:

"Whilst preparing for the selection process I have to admit that I wasn't very good at the practice AST questions that the RAF provides on their website. In order to improve I embarked on a structured development programme where I would carry out 60 minutes intensive training in my weak areas every night after college. I soon began to notice an improvement and before I knew it I was finding the sample tests a lot easier and I could work through them quicker. I believe I am a driven and determined person who always looks to improve. You can never stop learning."

BEING SELF RELIANT AND RESPONSIBLE

Being self reliant involves, amongst other things, getting yourself up for work or school every morning, doing your own washing and ironing, and generally looking after yourself without the assistance of others, such as your parents. When you embark on your initial RAF training course you will need to be 100% self reliant and that includes getting up early in the morning and being at the right place at the right time. During your training and throughout your career in the RAF you will be required to take on responsible tasks. Depending on your choice of career these will include looking after hi-tech equipment and being responsible for personal administration. During the selection interview provide examples of where you already hold responsibility either at home, at school or at work. You should also provide evidence of where you are, or have been, self reliant.

HOW YOU REACT TO DISCIPLINE INCLUDING YOUR REACTION TO REGIMENTATION AND ROUTINE

Many people react badly to discipline, whether it's at home, during their education or even at work. In simple terms, they don't like being told what to do. This is something you'll have to get used to, not just in your RAF career but also in any future jobs and careers. The RAF recruitment staff may assess your attitude towards people in positions of authority such as your boss at work, police officers, your teachers and even your parents. Those applicants who demonstrate disrespect towards people in positions of authority will score poorly. After all, if you cannot respect people in positions of authority now, then there is little chance of you respecting the officers and senior members of the Royal Air Force when you sign up.

YOUR KNOWLEDGE OF THE RAF

I can guarantee that the recruitment staff will want to know what you have done to find out about the service and also your choice of career(s) during the selection process. There are a number of ways that you can improve your knowledge of both the service and your career choices and these include the following:

- Visiting the RAF website at www.raf.mod.uk;
- Reading your recruitment literature;
- Speaking to the Armed Forces Careers Office staff;
- Visiting an RAF establishment or museum.

During your preparation for selection I would recommend you factor into your action plan some study time that is centred on improving your knowledge of the RAF, its history, your chosen career, RAF establishments, RAF structure and aircraft/equipment.

HOW MOTIVATED YOU ARE TO JOIN THE RAF

Do you want to join the RAF or do you really want to join the RAF? When I applied to join the Armed Forces a number of years ago I couldn't wait to join and I worked really hard to pass each stage. Even when I failed the medical the first time around I didn't let this stop me from succeeding. During the interviews for joining, you will be able to demonstrate your motivation by:

- Dressing smart every time you attend the AFCO and presenting yourself in a positive manner;
- Carrying out lots of targeted preparation and then telling the recruitment staff how hard you have been working;
- Taking positive steps to improve on your weak areas;
- Providing evidence during the selection process of where you can meet the assessable qualities.

Every time you attend the AFCO or communicate with the recruitment staff your natural enthusiasm for joining should always shine through.

YOUR PERSONAL CIRCUMSTANCES

When you eventually join the RAF and embark on your initial training course the last thing you will need are any negative external distractions. Examples of these include:

- Parents or partners who do not support you in your application;
- Financial difficulties;
- A lack of physical fitness;

The RAF recruitment staff will assess you both during the application form stage and also during the interview. If you have any concerns that relate to your personal circumstances be sure to discuss them with the AFCO advisor. You will find them very supportive.

In order to measure how currently effective you are in each of the assessable qualities, look at the following table and place a circle around the number which you believe reflects you best in each of the different areas. For example, scoring yourself as a 5 in 'knowledge of the RAF' means that you are fully confident you could answer questions competently in this subject area. A score of 1 means you have plenty of work to do in this area. Finally, in the 'notes' box on the right hand side of each assessable area, write here what action you intend to take in order to improve.

TABLE OF ASSESSABLE QUALITIES – AN ACTION PLAN FOR IMPROVEMENT

Personal Turnout & Hygiene	1	2	3	4	5	
Physically active & physically fit	1	2	3	4	5	
Effective team member	1	2	3	4	5	
Maturity & professionalism	1	2	3	4	5	
Drive & determination to succeed	1	2	3	4	5	
Self reliant & responsible	1	2	3	4	5	
Reaction to discipline & regimentation	1	2	3	4	5	
Knowledge of the RAF & chosen career	1	2	3	4	5	
Motivational levels	1	2	3	4	5	
Personal circumstances	1	2	3	4	5	

Once you've completed the table you will now have an action plan and a good idea of what you need to do in order to improve in each area.

CHAPTER FIVE

THE AIRMAN/AIRWOMAN SELECTION TEST (AST)

During the initial stages of the RAF selection process you will be required to sit what is called the Airman/Airwoman Selection Test or AST as it is otherwise called. It consists of a number of different aptitude tests, which are designed to assess which careers in the RAF you are most suited to. There are many different career opportunities available and each one requires a different level of skill. The AST consists of seven timed multiple choice aptitude tests as follows:

- A verbal reasoning test which assesses how well you can interpret written information. During this test you will have 15 minutes to answer 20 questions;
- A numerical reasoning test which determines how accurately you can interpret numerical information such as charts, graphs and tables. The test will also assess your ability to use fractions, decimals and different

formulae. There are two parts to this test. During the first test you will have just 4 minutes to answer 12 questions that are based on fractions, decimals and formulae. During the second test you will have 11 minutes to answer 15 questions that relate to different graphs and tables;

- A work rate test which is used to assess how quickly and accurately you can carry out routine tasks. During this test you will have 4 minutes to answer 20 questions;
- A spatial reasoning test designed to examine your ability to work with different shapes and objects. During this test you will have just 4 minutes to answer 10 questions;
- A mechanical comprehension test which is used to assess how effectively you can work with different mechanical concepts. During this particular test you will have 10 minutes in which to answer 20 questions;
- An electrical comprehension test which will assess your ability to work with different electrical concepts. During this test you will have 11 minutes to complete 21 questions.
- A memory test which determines how accurately you can remember and recall information. There are two parts to this test and you will have a total of 10 minutes in which to answer 20 questions.

Within this section of the guide I will provide you with a number of hints, tips and practice questions to help you prepare for the real AST. Please note that the questions provided are not the exact questions you'll encounter on your actual test day. The times that I have provided for each test are also different to the real AST. In addition to the tests provided within this booklet there are many different ways in which you can improve your scores on the day. These include:

- Consider purchasing a 'psychometric test' booklet. This will give you further practice with sample test questions and it will increase your knowledge and ability on each specific test area. You can buy these from www.how2become.co.uk where there is also an 'Armed Forces Selection Tests' booklet available.
- Drink plenty of water in the days leading up to the test. This will ensure that your concentration levels are at their best. If you are dehydrated then you are less likely to perform at your peak.
- Make sure you get a good night's sleep before the actual test. You will find that your performance will be much better if you are alert.
- Practise without a calculator. You may not be able to use one on the actual test day, so practising without one will prepare you beforehand.
- The tests usually take place at the Royal Air Force Careers Office. Make sure you get to the venue with plenty of time to spare. You are better off arriving 30 minutes early than 5 minutes late. Being late for the test will only make you more nervous.
- You do not need to take any writing implements with you on the day. The RAF Careers Office will provide you with any pens, paper or other stationery equipment required.

Now let's take a look at each of the different testing areas.

VERBAL REASONING TEST

During the Airman/Airwoman Selection Test you will be required to sit a verbal reasoning test. This test will assess how well you can interpret written information.

On the following pages you will find a number of practice verbal reasoning tests to assist you during your preparation. If, during the real test you find yourself struggling with a question, simply move on to the next one, but remember to leave the answer sheet blank for the particular question that you have not answered. If you then have time at the end, go back to the question(s) you have left and have another go. If you are still unable to answer the question then it is always worth 'guessing' as you still have a '1 in 5' chance of getting it right. In the real test you won't have much time to complete the questions so you must work quickly and accurately.

Take a look at the exercises on the following pages. Allow yourself 15 minutes to answer the 15 questions. Write your answer down in the box provided.

VERBAL REASONING TEST EXERCISE 1

Read the following information before answering the questions

Car A is red in colour and has 11 months left on the current MOT. The tax is due in 4 months time. The car has a full service history and has completed 34,000 miles. The car has had 3 owners.

Car B is black in colour and has a full 12 months MOT. The tax is not due for another 12 months. The car has completed 3,445 miles and has only had 1 owner. There is a full service history with the car.

Car C is red in colour and has no tax. The MOT is due to run out in 12 weeks time and the car has no service history. The speedometer reading is 134,000 miles and the car has had a total of 11 owners.

Car D is black in colour and has 11 months left on the current MOT. The tax is due in 6 months time. The car has no service history and has completed 34,000 miles. The car has only had 1 owner.

Car E is red in colour and has 7 months tax. The MOT runs out in 7 months time. The car has a partial service history and has completed 97,000 miles. It has had a total of 4 owners.

Question 1

You want a car that is red in colour and has a full service history with less than 100,000 miles. Which car would you choose?

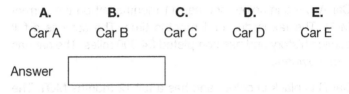

A.	B.	C.	D.	E.
Car A	Car B	Car C	Car D	Car E

Answer

Question 2

You want a car that has more than 6 months tax. You are not concerned about the colour but you also want 12 months MOT. Which car would you choose?

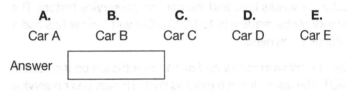

A.	B.	C.	D.	E.
Car A	Car B	Car C	Car D	Car E

Answer

Question 3

You want a car that is red in colour and has had no more than 4 owners. You want a minimum of 6 months tax. The mileage is irrelevant but you do want at least 7 months MOT. Which car would you choose?

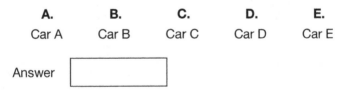

A.	B.	C.	D.	E.
Car A	Car B	Car C	Car D	Car E

Answer

VERBAL REASONING TEST EXERCISE 2

FLIGHT A, outbound, leaves at 8am and arrives at 1pm. The cost of the flight is £69 but this does not include a meal or refreshments. The return flight departs at 3am and arrives at its destination at 8am.

FLIGHT B, outbound, leaves at 3pm and arrives at 8pm. The cost of the flight is £97 and this includes a meal and refreshments. The return flight departs at 1pm and arrives at its destination at 5pm.

FLIGHT C, outbound, leaves at 4pm and arrives at 10pm. The cost of the flight is £70 but this does not include a meal or refreshments. The return flight departs at 10am and arrives at its destination at 4pm.

FLIGHT D, outbound, leaves at midnight and arrives at 3am. The cost of the flight is £105, which does include a meal and refreshments. The return flight departs at 3pm and arrives at 6pm.

FLIGHT E, outbound, leaves at 5am and arrives at 12noon. The cost of the flight is £39, which includes a meal and refreshments. The return flight departs at 5pm and arrives at its destination at midnight.

Question 1

You want a flight where the outbound flight arrives before 2pm on the day of departure. You don't want to pay any more than £50. Which flight would you choose?

A.	B.	C.	D.	E.
Flight A	Flight B	Flight C	Flight D	Flight E

Answer

Question 2

You don't want to pay more than £100 for the flight. You want a meal and the outbound departure time must be in the afternoon. Which flight would you choose?

A.	B.	C.	D.	E.
Flight A	Flight B	Flight C	Flight D	Flight E

Answer

Question 3

You want a return flight that departs in the afternoon between 12noon and 6pm. The cost of the flight must be below £100 and you do want a meal. The return flight must arrive at your destination before 6pm. Which flight would you choose?

A.	B.	C.	D.	E.
Flight A	Flight B	Flight C	Flight D	Flight E

Answer

VERBAL REASONING TEST EXERCISE 3

Janet and Steve have been married for 27 years. They have a daughter called Jessica who is 25 years old. They all want to go on holiday together but cannot make up their minds where to go. Janet's first choice would be somewhere hot and sunny abroad. Her second choice would be somewhere in their home country that involves a sporting activity. She does not like hill climbing or walking holidays but her third choice would be a skiing holiday. Steve's first choice would be a walking holiday in the hills somewhere in their home country and his second choice would be a sunny holiday abroad. He does not enjoy skiing. Jessica's first choice would be a skiing holiday and her second choice would be a sunny holiday abroad. Jessica's third choice would be a walking holiday in the hills of their home country.

Question 1

Which holiday are all the family most likely to go on together?

A.	**B.**	**C.**	**D.**	**E.**
Skiing	Walking	Holiday Abroad	Sporting activity holiday	Cannot say

Answer

Question 2

If Steve and Jessica were to go on holiday together where would they be most likely to go?

A.	**B.**	**C.**	**D.**	**E.**
Sunny Holiday Abroad	Skiing	Cannot say	Sporting activity holiday	Walking

Answer

Question 3

Which holiday are Janet and Steve most likely to go on together?

A.	B.	C.	D.	E.
Cannot say	Walking	Sporting activity holiday	Skiing	Sunny Holiday Abroad

Answer

VERBAL REASONING TEST EXERCISE 4

Barry and Bill work at their local supermarket in the town of Whiteham. Barry works every day except Wednesdays. The supermarket is run by Barry's brother Elliot who is married to Sarah. Sarah and Elliot have 2 children called Marcus and Michelle who are both 7 years old and they live in the road adjacent to the supermarket. Barry lives in a town called Redford, which is 7 miles from Whiteham. Bill's girlfriend Maria works in a factory in her hometown of Brownhaven. The town of Redford is 4 miles from Whiteham and 6 miles from the seaside town of Tenford. Sarah and Elliot take their children on holiday to Tenford twice a year and Barry usually gives them a lift in his car. Barry's mum lives in Tenford and he tries to visit her once a week at 2pm when he is not working.

Question 1

Which town does Elliot live in?

A.	**B.**	**C.**	**D.**	**E.**
Redford	Whiteham	Brownhaven	Tenford	Cannot say

Answer

Question 2

On which day of the week does Barry visit his mother?

A.	**B.**	**C.**	**D.**	**E.**
Cannot say	Monday	Tuesday	Wednesday	Thursday

Answer

Question 3
Bill and Maria live together in Brownhaven.

A.	**B.**	**C.**
True	False	Cannot say

Answer

VERBAL REASONING TEST EXERCISE 5

FLAT A is located in a town. It is 12 miles from the nearest train station. It has 2 bedrooms and is located on the ground floor. The monthly rental is £450 and the council tax is £50 per month. The lease is for 6 months.

FLAT B is located in the city centre and is 2 miles from the nearest train station. It is located on the 3rd floor. The monthly rental is £600 and the council tax is £130 per month. The lease is for 6 months and it has 3 bedrooms.

FLAT C is located in the city centre and is 3 miles from the nearest train station. It is located on the 1st floor and has 1 bedroom. The monthly rental is £550 and the council tax is £100 per month. The lease is for 12 months.

FLAT D is located in a town. The monthly rental is £395 per month and the council tax is £100 per month. It is located on the ground floor and the lease is for 6 months. It is 18 miles from the nearest train station. The flat has 2 bedrooms.

FLAT E is located in a village and is 12 miles from the nearest train station. It has 3 bedrooms and is located on the 2nd floor. The monthly rental is £375 and the council tax is £62.

Question 1

You want a flat that is within 10 miles of the nearest train station and is located on the 1st floor or lower. The combined monthly rent/council tax bill must be no greater than £600. Which flat would you choose?

A.	**B.**	**C.**	**D.**	**E.**
Flat A	Flat B	Flat C	Flat D	None of the above

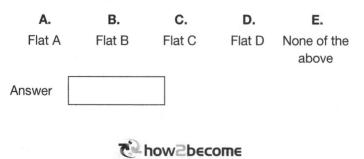

Answer

Question 2

You want a flat that has at least 2 bedrooms and has a combined monthly rent/council tax bill that does not exceed £450. Which flat would you choose?

A.	**B.**	**C.**	**D.**	**E.**
Flat A	Flat B	Flat C	Flat D	Flat E

Answer

Question 3

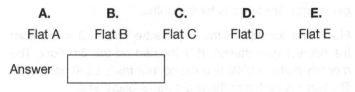

You want a flat that has a combined monthly rent/council tax bill that is not in excess of £600, is within 20 miles of the nearest train station and has a lease of at least 6 months. Which flat would you choose?

A.	**B.**	**C.**	**D.**	**E.**
Flat A	Flat B	Flat C	Flat D	Flat E

Answer

ANSWERS TO VERBAL REASONING TESTS

Verbal reasoning test 1

1. A
2. B
3. E

Verbal reasoning test 2

1. E
2. B
3. B

Verbal reasoning test 3

1. C
2. A
3. E

Verbal reasoning test 4

1. B
2. D
3. C

Verbal reasoning test 5

1. E
2. E
3. A & D

NUMERICAL REASONING TESTS

During the Airman/Airwoman Selection Test you will be required to undertake a numerical reasoning test. This test is used to determine how accurately you can interpret numerical information such as charts, graphs and tables. The test will also assess your ability to use fractions, decimals and different formulae. As you can imagine, the most effective way to prepare for this type of test is to carry out lots of sample numerical reasoning test questions, without the aid of a calculator.

During the actual numerical reasoning test with the RAF you will have a specific amount of time to answer each question. It is important that you do not spend too much time on one particular question. Remember that the clock is ticking. Have a go at the first numerical reasoning exercise on the following page and use a blank sheet of paper to work out your calculations. Remember to check your answers very carefully. It is important that you check any incorrect answers to see why you got them wrong.

You have 10 minutes in which to answer the 20 questions. Calculators are not permitted.

NUMERICAL REASONING TEST EXERCISE 1

Question 1

Calculate 5.99 + 16.02

A.	B.	C.	D.	E.
19.01	20.01	21.99	22.99	22.01

Answer

Question 2

Calculate 3.47 – 1.20

A.	B.	C.	D.	E.
22.7	2.27	1.27	2.67	0.27

Answer

Question 3

Calculate 98.26 – 62.89

A.	B.	C.	D.	E.
37.35	35.37	36.35	36.37	37.73

Answer

Question 4

Calculate 45.71 – 29.87

A.	B.	C.	D.	E.
14.84	18.88	14.89	15.84	15.85

Answer

Question 5
Calculate 564.87 + 321.60

A.	B.	C.	D.	E.
886.45	886.74	886.47	868.47	868.74

Answer

Question 6
Calculate 16.0 – 9.9

A.	B.	C.	D.	E.
6.9	6.1	7.1	7.9	5.1

Answer

Question 7
Calculate 1109.12 + 0.8

A.	B.	C.	D.	E.
1109.20	1109.92	1109.02	1110.20	1110.92

Answer

Question 8
Calculate 4.1 × 3.0

A.	B.	C.	D.	E.
123	9.1	12.41	7.1	12.3

Answer

Question 9

Calculate 16.8 × 4

A.	**B.**	**C.**	**D.**	**E.**
67.2	64.8	47.1	67.4	67.8

Answer

Question 10

Calculate 2.2 × 2.2

A.	**B.**	**C.**	**D.**	**E.**
4.4	44.4	2.84	4.84	8.44

Answer

Question 11

In the following question what is the value of *t*?

$$\frac{5\,(t - 32)}{2} = 5$$

Answer

Question 12

In the following question what is the value of *t*?

$$\frac{3\,(t + 35)}{6} = 35$$

Answer

Question 13

In the following question what is the value of *t*?

$$\frac{9\ (t \times 16)}{5} = 144$$

Answer

Question 14

In the following question what is the value of *t*?

$$\frac{4t - 16)}{32} = 2$$

Answer

Question 15

Convert 0.7 to a fraction

A.	B.	C.	D.	E.
$\frac{7}{10}$	$\frac{3}{4}$	$\frac{75}{1}$	$\frac{1}{10}$	$\frac{2}{3}$

Answer

Question 16

Convert 2.5 to a fraction

A.	B.	C.	D.	E.
$\frac{25}{10}$	$\frac{3}{6}$	$2\frac{1}{2}$	$\frac{1}{25}$	$2\frac{2}{1}$

Answer

Question 17

Convert 3.75 to a fraction

A.	B.	C.	D.	E.
$\frac{75}{1}$	$\frac{1}{375}$	$3\frac{1}{75}$	$\frac{75}{3}$	$3\frac{3}{4}$

Answer

Question 18

Convert $\frac{3}{10}$ to a decimal

A.	B.	C.	D.	E.
3.0	0.3	3.33	0.03	0.003

Answer

Question 19

Convert $\frac{1}{4}$ to a decimal

A.	B.	C.	D.	E.
0.025	2.5	0.25	0.4	4.0

Answer

Question 20

Convert $\frac{4}{5}$ to a decimal

A.	B.	C.	D.	E.
0.08	8.0	4.5	5.4	0.8

Answer

ANSWERS TO NUMERICAL REASONING TEST EXERCISE 1

1. E
2. B
3. B
4. D
5. C
6. B
7. E
8. E
9. A
10. D
11. 34
12. 35
13. 5
14. 20
15. A
16. C
17. E
18. B
19. C
20. E

NUMERICAL REASONING TEST EXERCISE 2

On the following pages I have supplied you with a number of practice numerical reasoning tests which will improve your ability to use tables and graphs. If you find yourself struggling with a question, move on to the next one but remember to leave the answer sheet blank for the particular question that you have not answered. If you then have time at the end, by all means go back to the questions you have left and try to answer them.

Allow yourself 15 minutes to answer the 15 questions. Write your answer down on a blank sheet of paper.

NUMERICAL REASONING TEST EXERCISE 2

Look at Table 1 below and then answer the questions on the following page.

TABLE 1. The following table lists the type of bonus each member of staff will receive if they reach a specific number of sales per hour they work. The table has not yet been completed. Staff work seven hour shifts. In order to answer the questions you will need to complete the table.

Time	10 Sales	20 Sales	30 Sales	40 Sales
1st hour	£21.00	£41.50	£60.50	£72.00
2nd hour	£18.00	£35.00	£52.00	£60.00
3rd hour	£15.00	£28.50	£43.50	£50.00
4th hour	-	£22.00	£35.00	£42.00
5th hour	£9.00	-	£26.50	£36.00
6th hour	£6.00	£9.00	-	£32.00
7th hour	£3.00	£3.50	£9.50	-

Note: If a worker achieves 160 sales or more during their 7 hour shift they will receive an additional £50 bonus.

Question 1

If the table was complete how much could a worker earn in bonuses if they reached 10 sales every hour of their 7 hour shift?

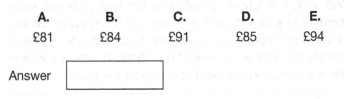

A.	B.	C.	D.	E.
£81	£84	£91	£85	£94

Answer

Question 2

How much would a worker earn in bonuses if they reached 30 sales per hour for the first 3 hours of their shift and 40 sales per hour for the remaining 4 hours of their shift?

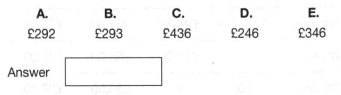

A.	B.	C.	D.	E.
£292	£293	£436	£246	£346

Answer

Question 3

How much would a worker earn in bonuses if they reached 10 sales during their first and last hour, 20 sales during the 2nd and 6th hours, 30 sales during the 3rd and 5th hours and 40 sales during the 4th hour?

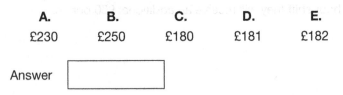

A.	B.	C.	D.	E.
£230	£250	£180	£181	£182

Answer

Look at the following bar chart below before answering the questions on the following page.

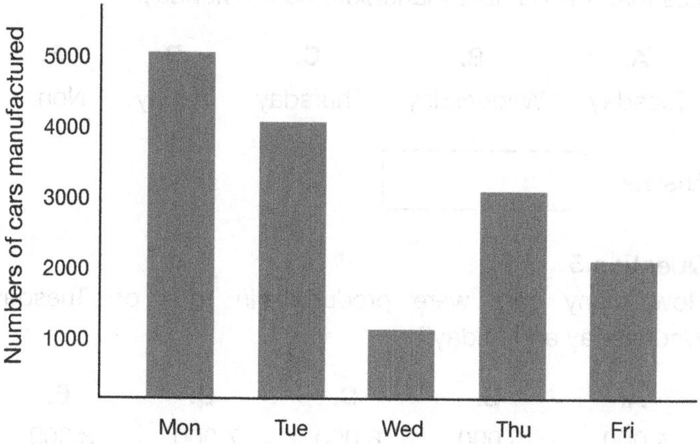

The above chart indicates the total number of cars manufactured per day of the week at the Arlingford Car Depot. Study the graph and answer the questions on the following page.

Question 4

On which day was the number of cars manufactured 80% less than the number manufactured on Monday?

A.	B.	C.	D.	E.
Tuesday	Wednesday	Thursday	Friday	None

Answer

Question 5

How many cars were produced in total on Tuesday, Wednesday and Friday?

A.	B.	C.	D.	E.
4,000	5,000	6,000	7,000	8,000

Answer

Question 6

What was the average number of cars manufactured per day for the working week?

A.	B.	C.	D.	E.
2,142	2,500	3,000	2,141	2,140

Answer

The following graph indicates the total monthly profits of four competing companies. Study the graph and answer the questions on the following page.

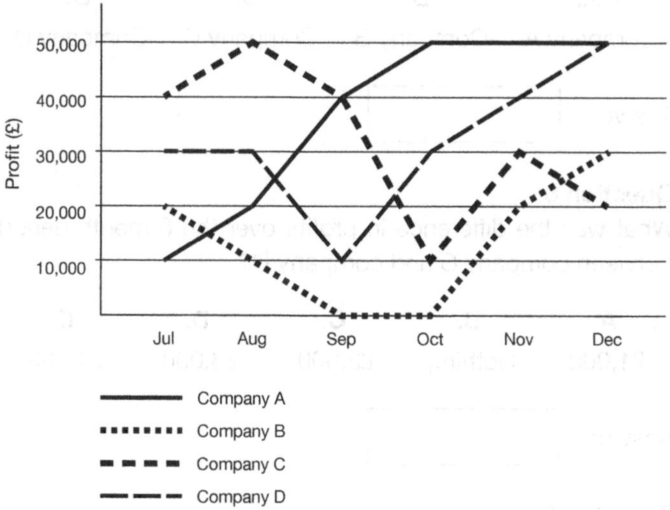

Question 7

Over the 6 month period, which company made the greatest profit?

A.	B.	C.	D.
Company A	Company B	Company C	Company D

Answer

Question 8

What was the difference in profits over the 6 month period between company C and company D?

A.	B.	C.	D.	E.
£1,000	Nothing	£2,000	£3,000	£4,000

Answer

Question 9

What was the total combined 6 month profit for all four companies?

A.	B.	C.	D.	E.
£660,000	£610,000	£630,000	£650,000	£690,000

Answer

The following table shows the distribution list for a UK based company including the location of delivery, type of package ordered, the quantity ordered and the cost excluding delivery. Study the table before answering the questions on the following page.

Date	Location of delivery	Package ordered	Quantity ordered	Cost (excluding delivery)
13th Jan	Kent	Package 1	2	£45
17th Jan	Preston	Package 4	13	£1,600
2nd Feb	Manchester	Package 2	6	£246
3rd Feb	Glasgow		12	£270
17th Feb	Fareham	Package 2	8	
19th Mar	Huddersfield	Package 5	1	£213
20th Mar	Crewe		3	£639

Question 10

Which package will be delivered on the 3rd of February?

A.	B.	C.	D.
Package 1	Package 2	Package 4	Package 5

Answer

Question 11

What will be the cost (excluding delivery) on the 17th of February?

A.	B.	C.	D.	E.
£322	£324	£326	£328	£330

Answer

Question 12

Which package is scheduled to be delivered to Crewe on the 20th of March?

A.	B.	C.	D.
Package 1	Package 2	Package 4	Package 5

Answer

The following bar chart indicates the total number of people employed by a large international distribution company. Study the chart before answering the questions on the following page.

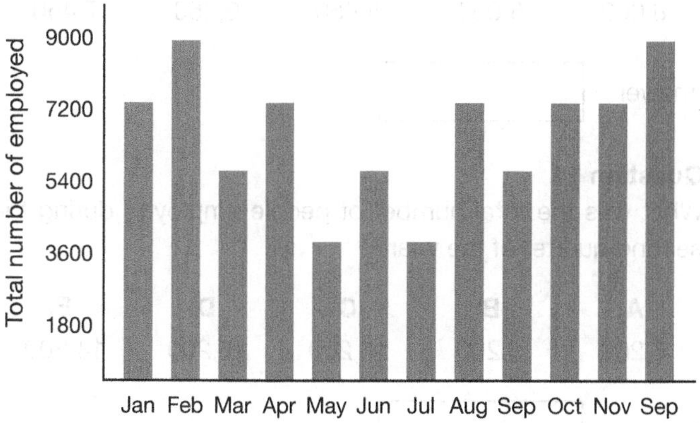

Question 13
What was the average monthly employment figure for the 12 month period?

A.	B.	C.	D.	E.
6,000	5,000	5,450	6,450	7,450

Answer

Question 14
What was the total number of people employed during the second quarter of the year?

A.	B.	C.	D.	E.
6,200	5,200	16,200	15,200	14,300

Answer

Question 15
What was the difference between the number of people employed in the first quarter and the last quarter of the year?

A.	B.	C.	D.	E.
1,800	1,700	1,600	18,000	17,000

Answer

ANSWERS TO NUMERIAL REASONING TEST EXERCISE 2

1. B
2. E
3. A
4. B
5. D
6. C
7. A
8. B
9. E
10. A
11. D
12. D
13. D
14. C
15. A

THE WORK RATE TEST

During the AST you will be required to undertake a work rate test. This form of test assesses your ability to work quickly and accurately whilst carrying out routine tasks; something which is integral to the role of an Airman/Airwoman.

Before we move on to the test questions, let's take a look at a sample question. To begin with, study the following box which contains different numbers, letters and symbols.

5	6	3	1	2	Numbers
J	F	T	S	W	Letters
◣	✚	☾	⬟	●	Symbols

↑ ↑ ↑ ↑ ↑

Columns

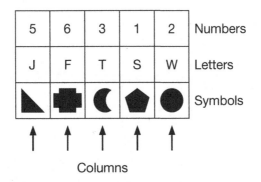

In the sample questions that I have provided you, you will be given a code consisting of numbers, letters or symbols. Your task is to look at the 5 provided alternative codes and decide which one has been taken from the *SAME* columns as the original code.

For example, look at the following code:

CODE A – 563

Now look at the 5 alternatives, which are taken from the above grid, and decide which code has been taken from the same columns as code A.

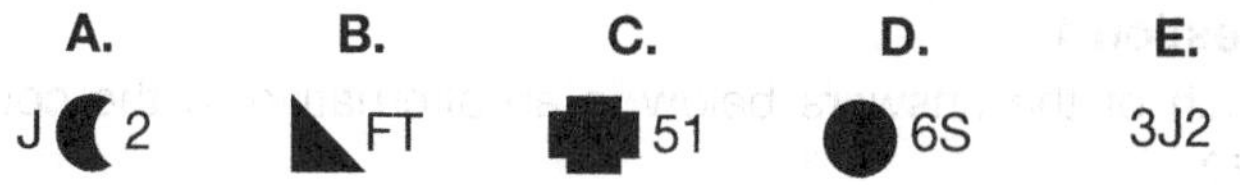

You can see that the answer is in fact B and the code FT. The reason for this is that this code has been taken from the same columns and in the **same order** as the original code.

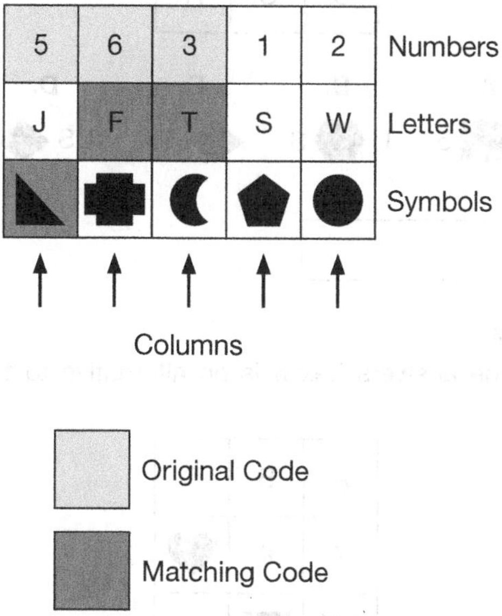

Now take the time to work through the following exercises. You have 10 minutes to work through the 15 questions. If you do not finish the test, try practising the questions you have missed in your own time. If you get any wrong, make sure you go back and understand why.

Question 1

Which of the answers below is an alternative to the code **765**?

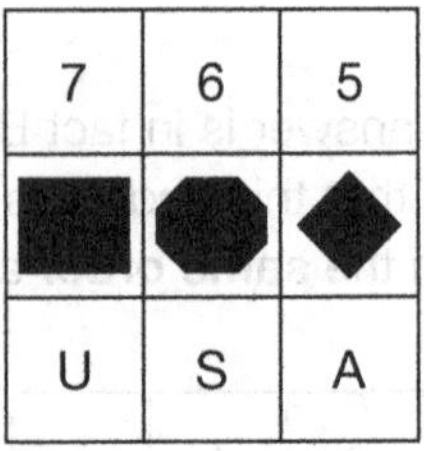

A.   B.   C.   D.

U ■ 5   U ⬡ S   ◆ 6U   US ◆

Answer [   ]

Question 2

Which of the answers below is an alternative to the code **A8♥**?

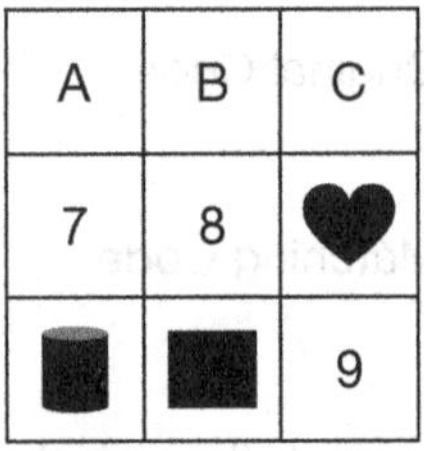

A.   B.   C.   D.

■ C9   78 ■   7B9   897

Answer [   ]

Question 3

Which of the answers below is an alternative to the code **YEF**?

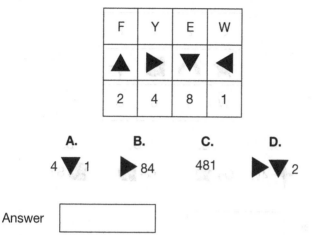

F	Y	E	W
▲	▶	▼	◀
2	4	8	1

A.	**B.**	**C.**	**D.**
4▼1	▶84	481	▶▼2

Answer

Question 4

Which of the answers below is an alternative to the code **178**?

A	B	C	Z
7	8	3	1
▼	▶	◀	▲

A.	**B.**	**C.**	**D.**
▲A3	Z▼3	▲AB	▶3Z

Answer

Question 5

Which of the answers below is an alternative to the code **82T**?

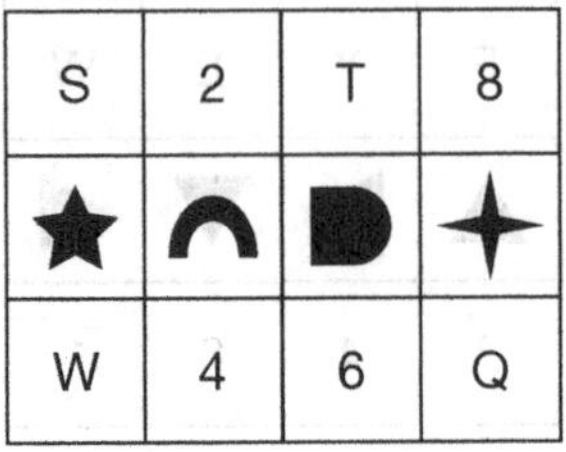

Answer

Question 6

Which of the answers below is an alternative to the code **X39**?

D	S	E	X
9	3	2	5
0	1	4	8

A.	**B.**	**C.**	**D.**
514	8S2	0S8	51D

Answer

Question 7

Which of the answers below is an alternative to the code **XWQ**?

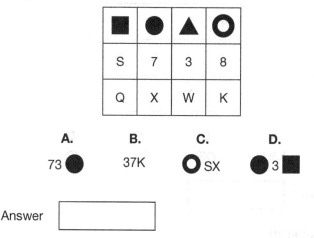

■	●	▲	○
S	7	3	8
Q	X	W	K

A. 73●

B. 37K

C. ○SX

D. ●3■

Answer

Question 8

Which of the answers below is an alternative to the code **482**?

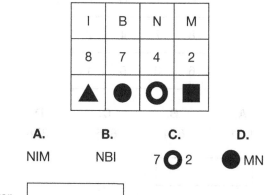

I	B	N	M
8	7	4	2
▲	●	○	■

A. NIM

B. NBI

C. 7○2

D. ●MN

Answer

Question 9

Which of the answers below is an alternative to the code **0W9**?

4	0	2	9
S	7	3	8
Q	X	W	K

A.	**B.**	**C.**	**D.**
X3Q	7X8	QS4	X28

Answer

Question 10

Which of the answers below is an alternative to the code **672**?

U	Z	R	E
8	7	4	2
6	3	5	1

A.	**B.**	**C.**	**D.**
U31	6Z4	8Z5	3E8

Answer

Question 11

Which of the answers below is an alternative to the code **3PJ**?

R	A	F	P
1	2	3	4
J	■	D	●

A.	B.	C.	D.
D ● A	14F	■ R3	D41

Answer

Question 12

Which of the answers below is an alternative to the code **72S**?

●	 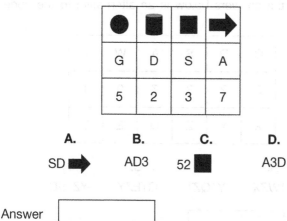	■	➡
G	D	S	A
5	2	3	7

A.	B.	C.	D.
SD ➡	AD3	52 ■	A3D

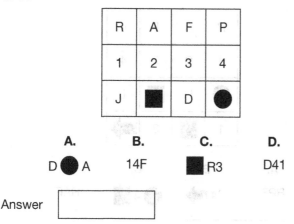

Answer

Question 13

Which of the answers below is an alternative to the code **1LS**?

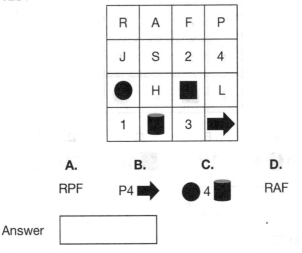

R	A	F	P
J	S	2	4
	H		L
1		3	

A. RPF

B. P4 

C.  4 

D. RAF

Answer

Question 14

Which of the answers below is an alternative to the code **X1W3D**?

G	D	S	A	W	L
5	2	3	7	0	1
X	Y	Z	Q	E	T

A. 51WZX

B. Y1QZT

C. GTEZY

D. YZ7SD

Answer

Question 15

Which of the answers below is an alternative to the code **J4F**?

R		F	P
J			4
	H		L
1		3	

A.	**B.**	**C.**	**D.**
1HF	RPL	31P	1L3

Answer

ANSWERS TO WORK RATE TEST

1. D
2. C
3. D
4. C
5. C
6. D
7. D
8. A
9. D
10. A
11. D
12. B
13. C
14. C
15. D

SPATIAL REASONING TESTS

During the Airman/Airwoman Selection Test you will be required to undertake a spatial reasoning test.

The definition of spatial reasoning is as follows:

'The ability to interpret and make drawings from mental images and visualise movement or change in those images.'

During the AST you will be confronted with a number of spatial reasoning questions and the only effective way to prepare for them is to practise as many as you can. You will find that the more questions you try, the quicker you will become at answering them. Although the examples I have provided in this section of the guide are timed, I would recommend that you take the time following the test to look at how the answers are reached. This is just as important as practising the tests under timed conditions.

Example question

Take a look] at the following 3 shapes. Note the letters on the side of each shape:

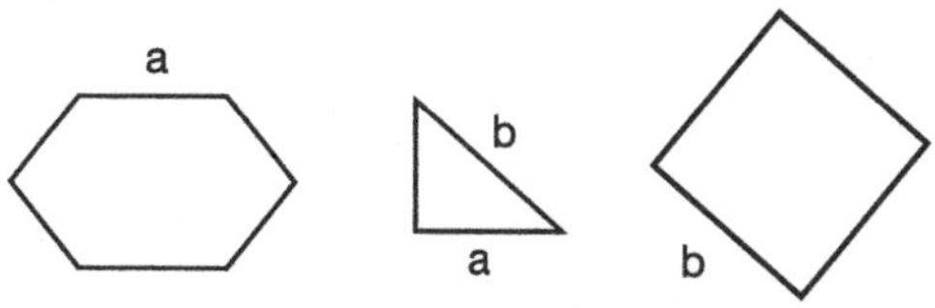

Join all of the 3 shapes together with the corresponding letters to make the following shape:

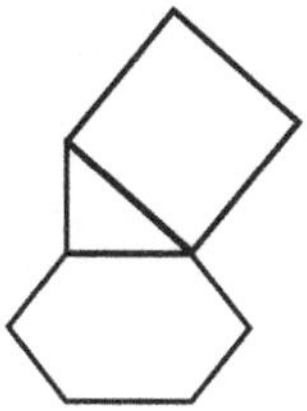

During the following spatial reasoning exercise your task is to look at the given shapes and decide which of the examples matches the shape when joined together by the corresponding letters. You have 3 minutes to answer the 8 questions.

SPATIAL REASONING TEST EXERCISE 1

Question 1

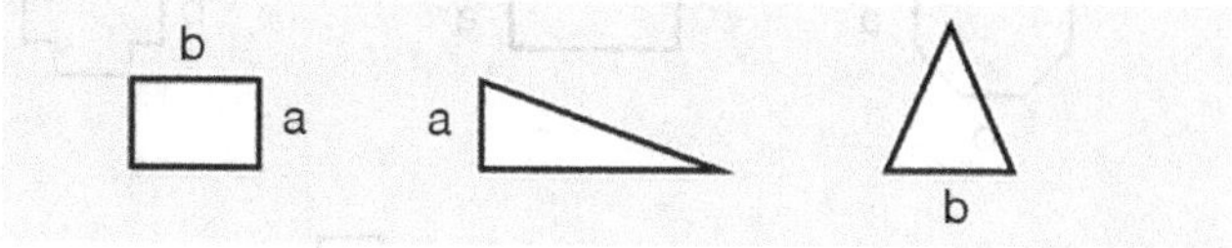

A.

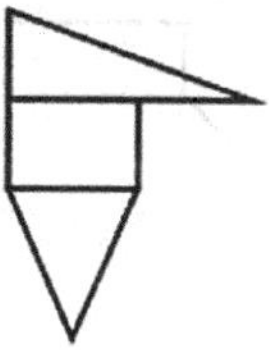

B.

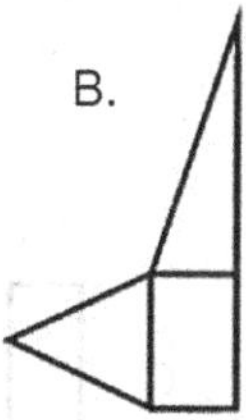

C.

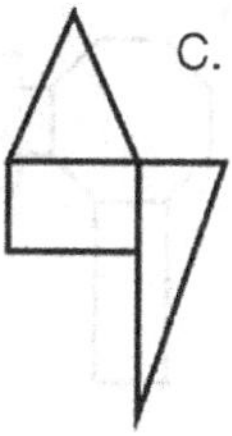

D.

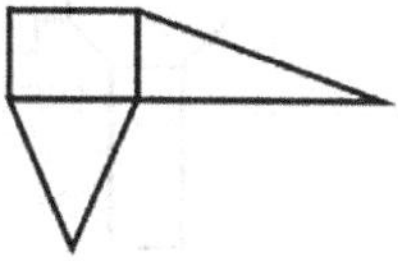

E.

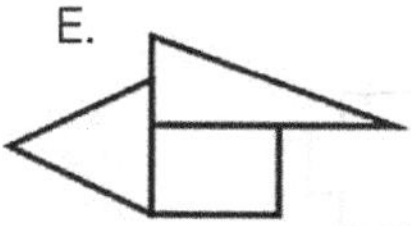

Answer

Question 2

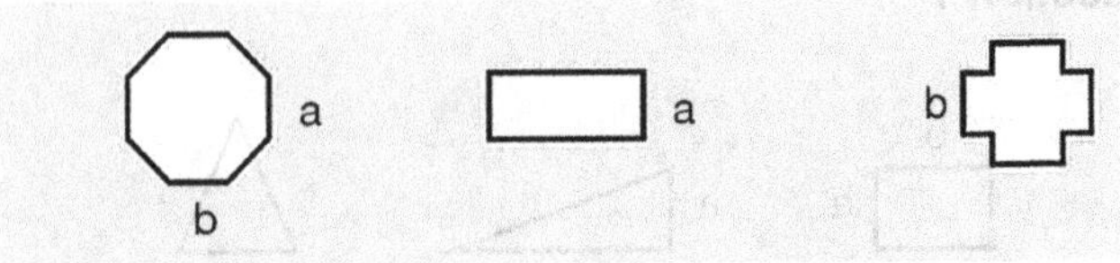

A.

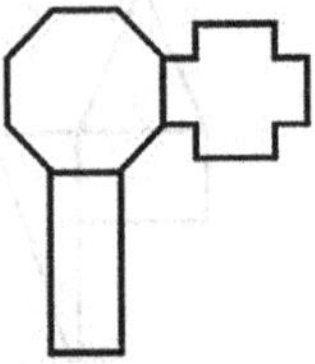

B.

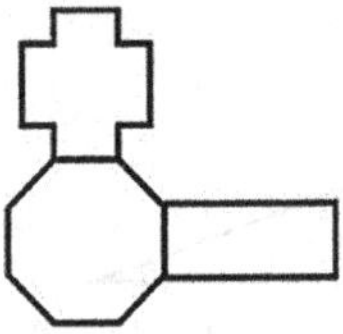

C.

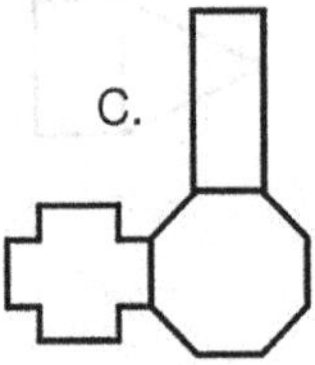

D.

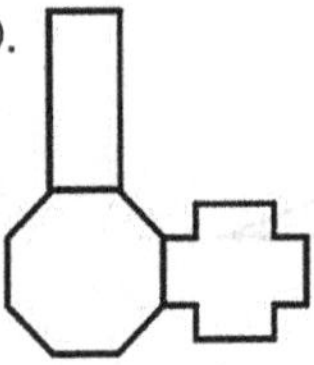

E.

Answer

Question 3

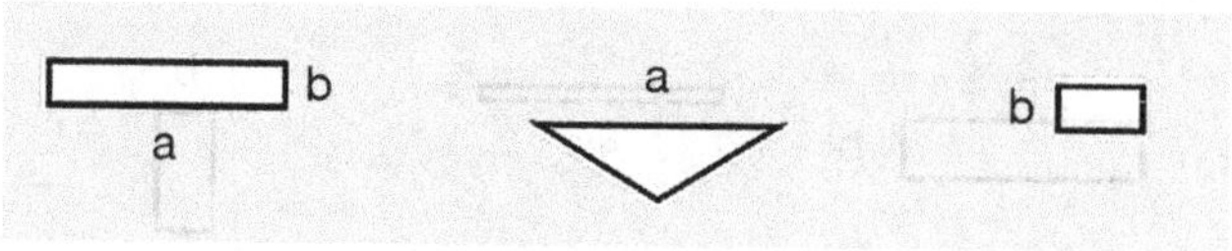

A.

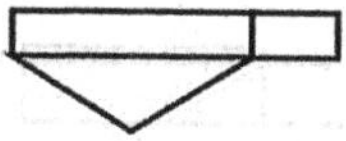

B.

D.

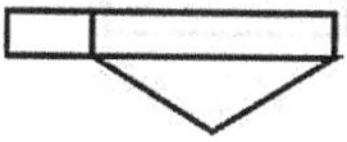

C.

E.

Answer

Question 4

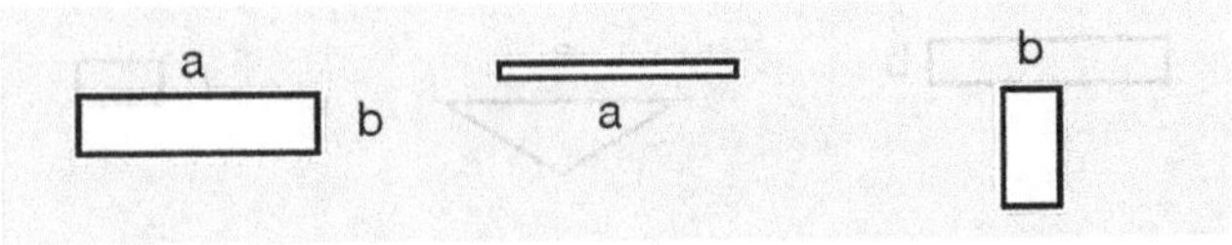

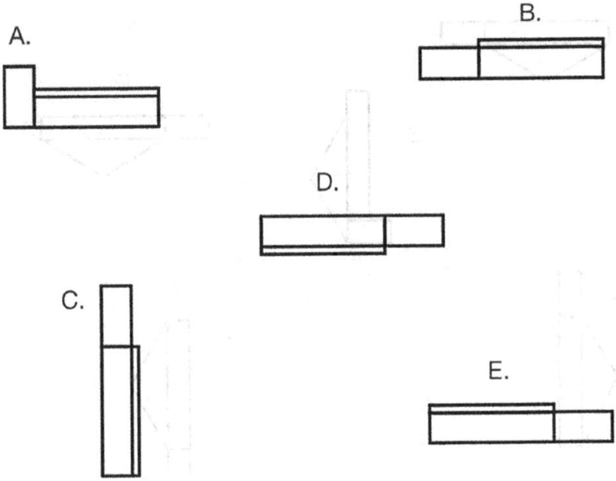

Answer

Question 5

A.

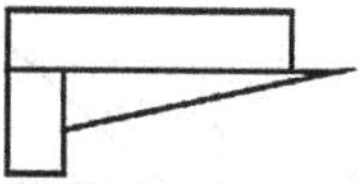

C.

B.

D.

E.

Answer

Question 6

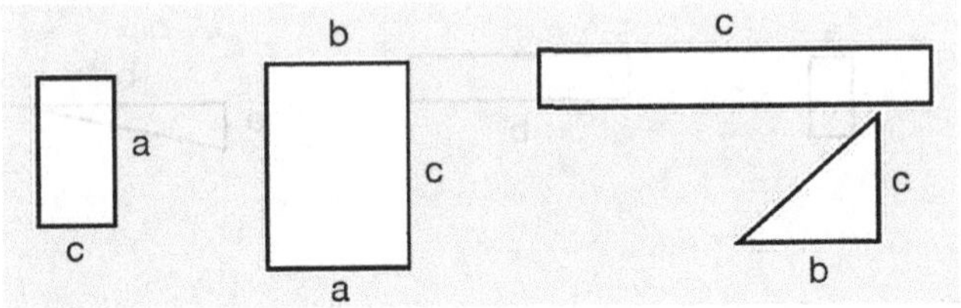

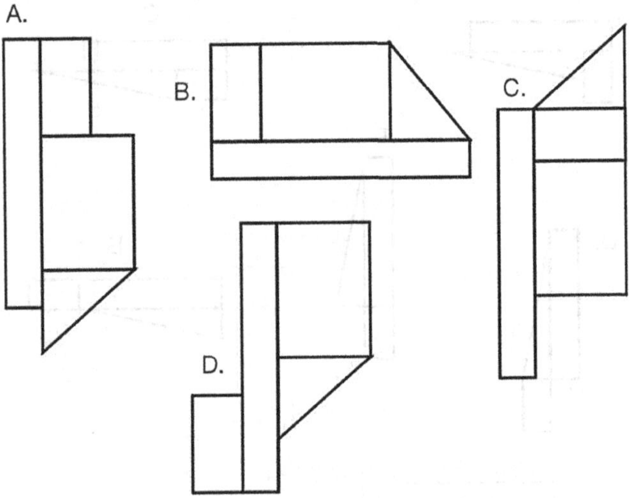

Answer

Question 7

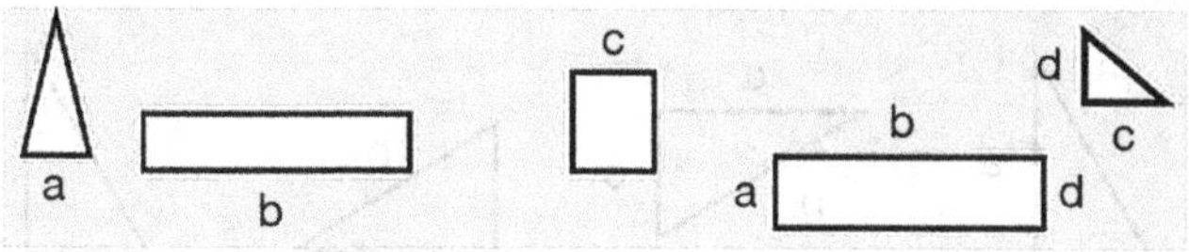

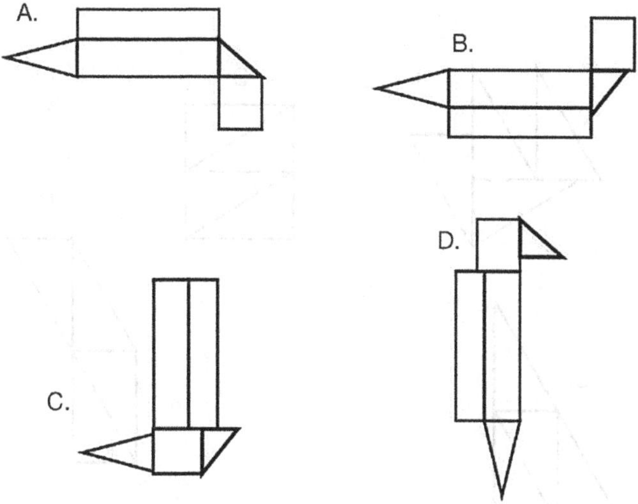

Answer

Question 8

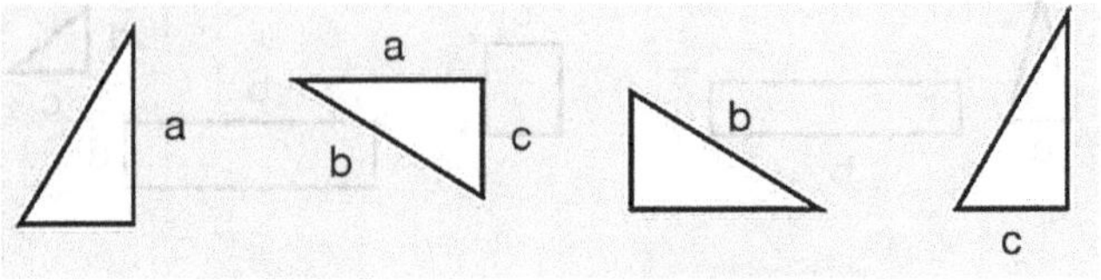

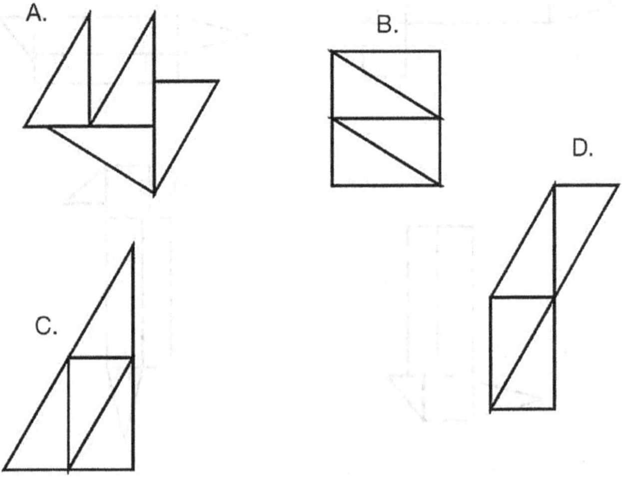

Answer

Now that you have completed the exercise take the time to work through your answers carefully. If you got any incorrect, make sure you understand how the correct answer is reached as this will assist you during your development.

ANSWERS TO SPATIAL REASONING TEST EXERCISE 1

1. B
2. D
3. A
4. E
5. D
6. B
7. A
8. C

SPATIAL REASONING TEST EXERCISE 2

During the second spatial reasoning test that I've provided you with you will be required to look at 3-dimensional objects. You have to imagine the 3-dimensional objects rotated in a specific way and then match them up against a choice of examples.

Look at the 2 objects below:

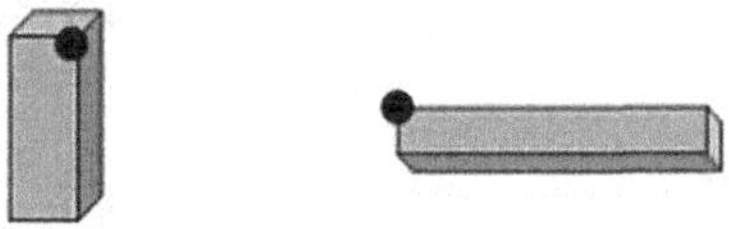

You now have to decide which of the 4 options provided demonstrates both objects rotated with the dot in the correct position. Look at the options below:

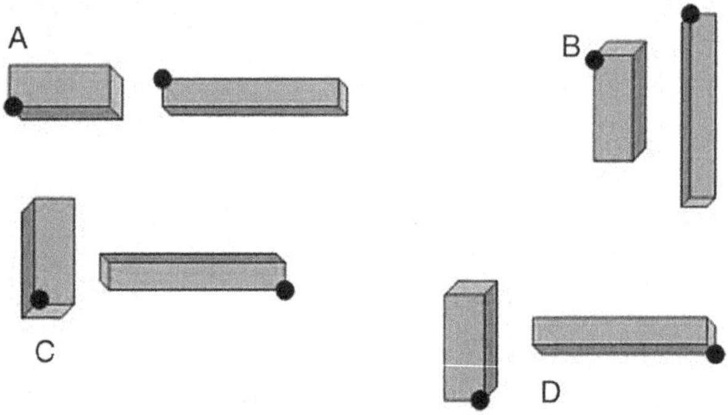

The correct answer is C

Now move on to spatial reasoning test exercise 2 on the following page. You have 3 minutes in which to complete the 8 questions.

SPATIAL REASONING TEST EXERCISE 2

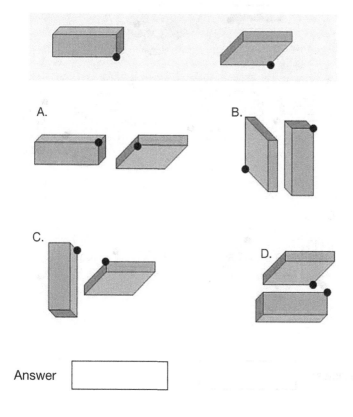

Question 1

A.

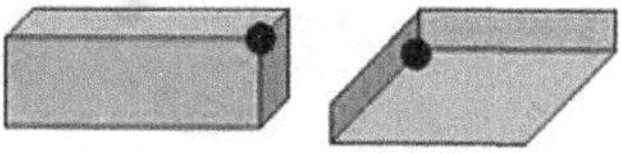

B.

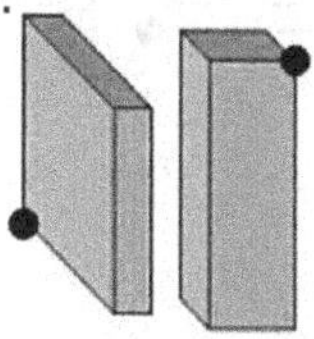

C.

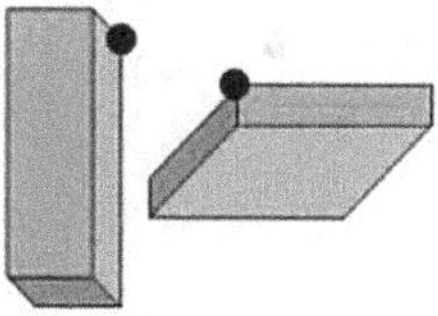

D.

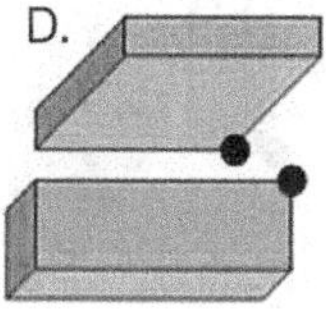

Answer

Question 2

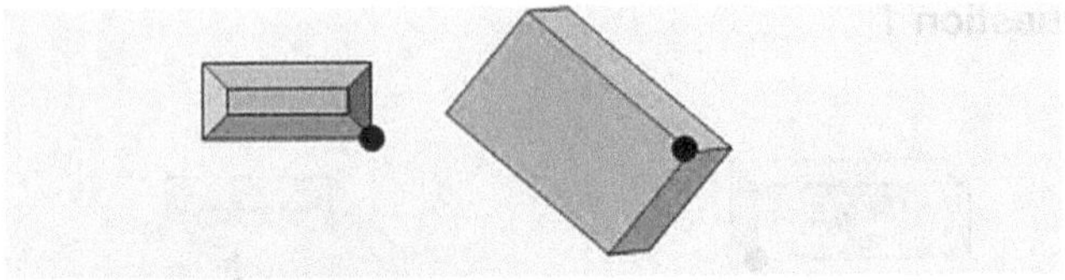

A.

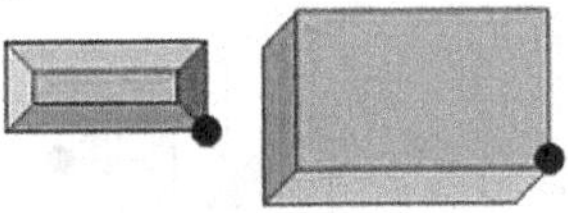

B.

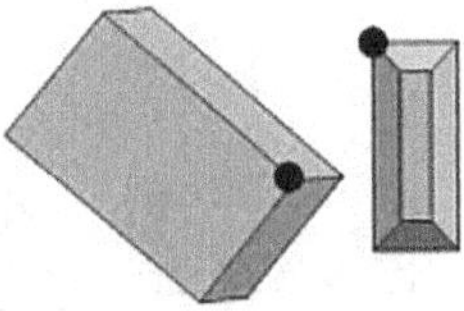

C.

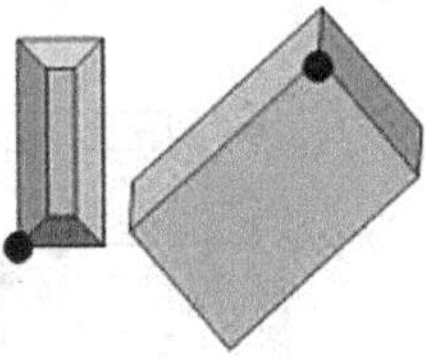

D.

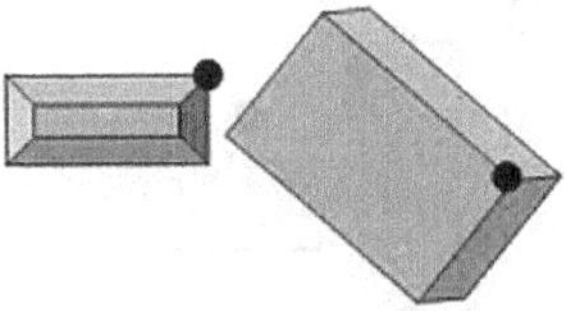

Answer

Question 3

A.

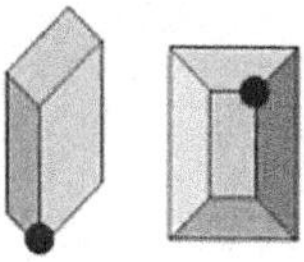

B.

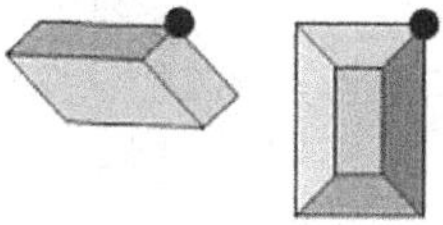

C.

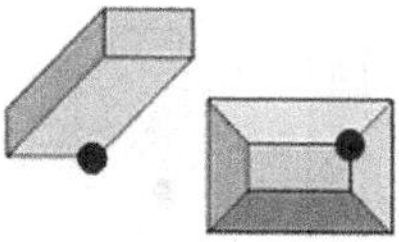

D.

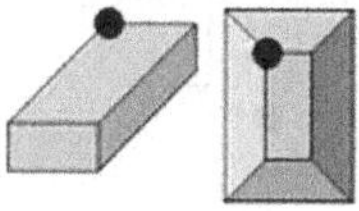

Answer

Question 4

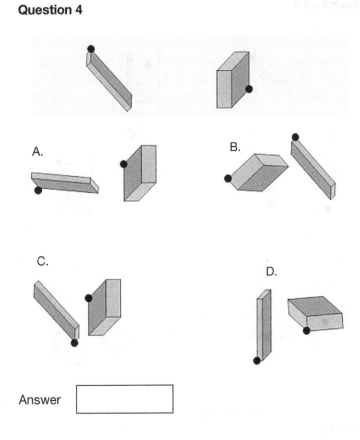

A.

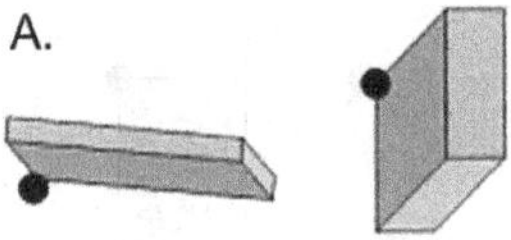

B.

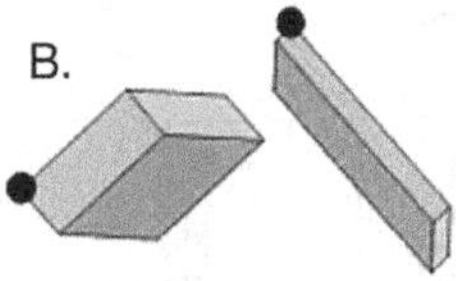

C.

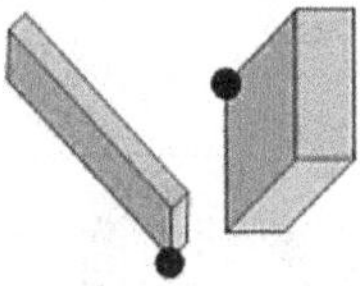

D.

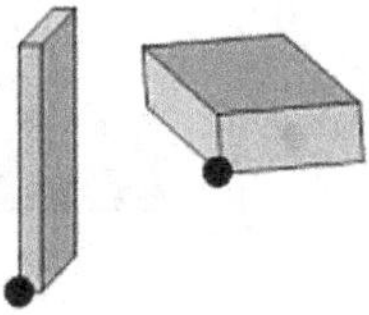

Answer

Question 5

A.

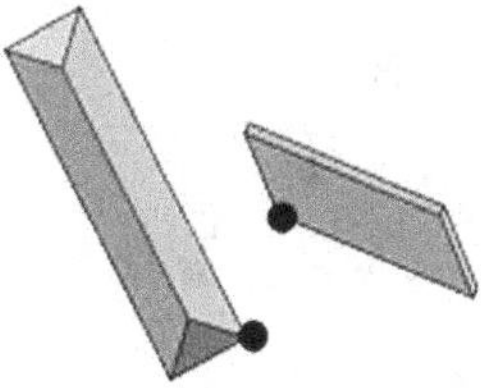

B.

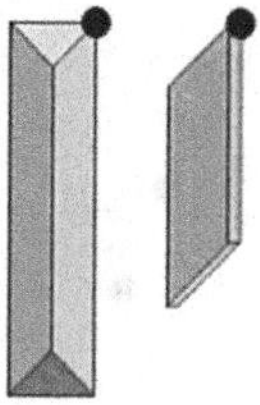

C.

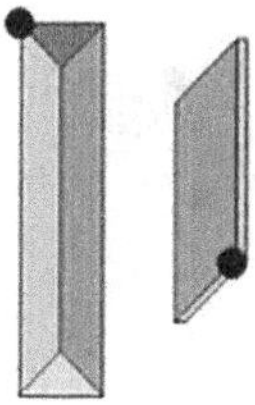

D.

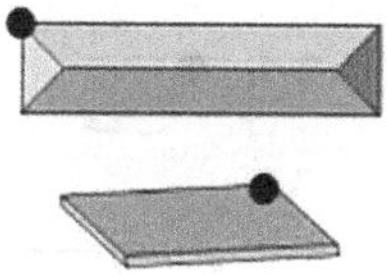

Answer

Question 6

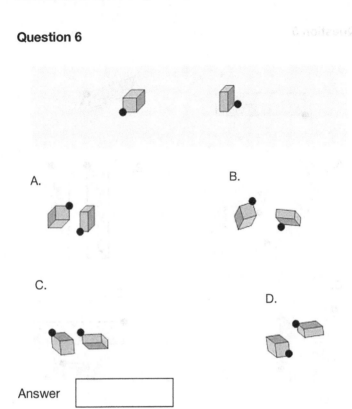

A.

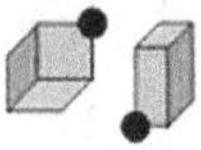

B.

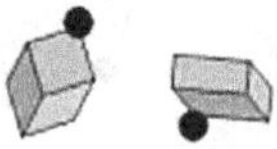

C.

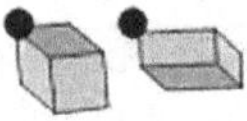

D.

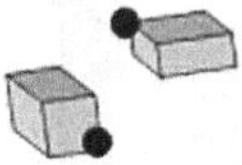

Answer

Question 7

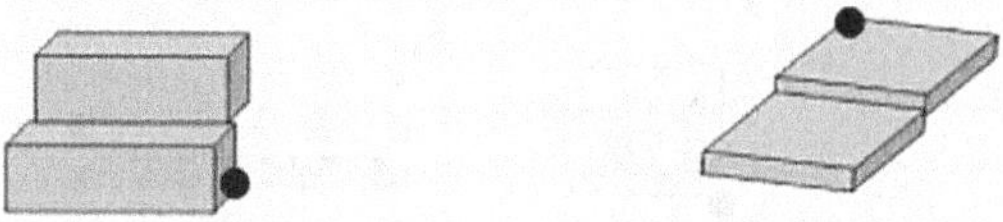

A.

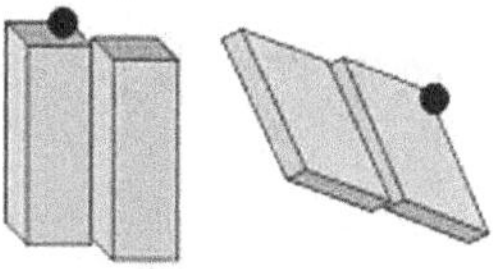

B.

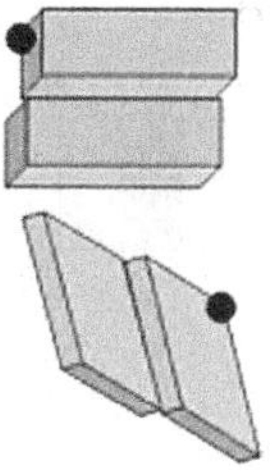

C.

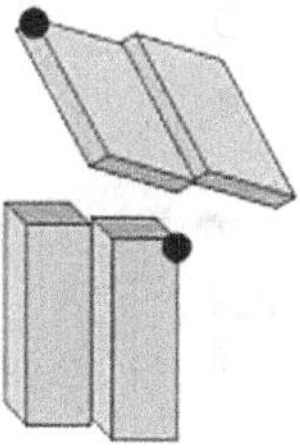

D.

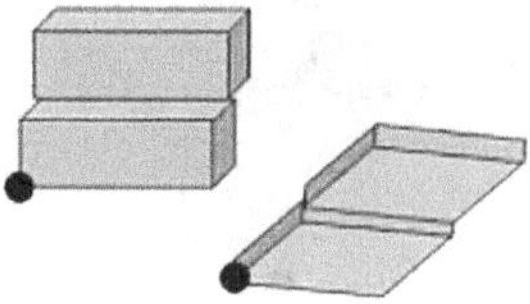

Answer

Question 8

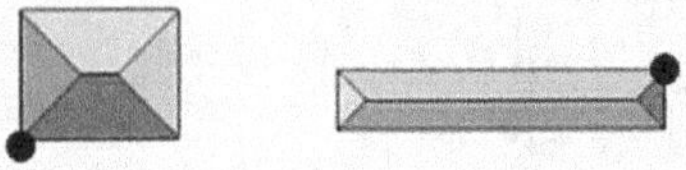

A.

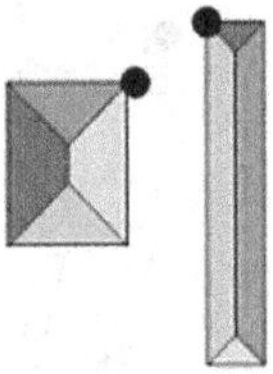

B.

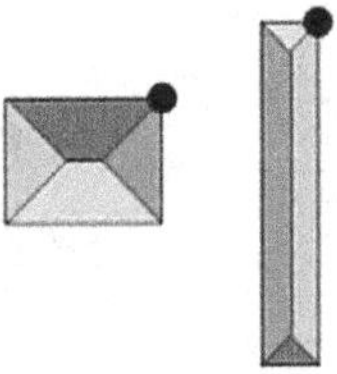

C.

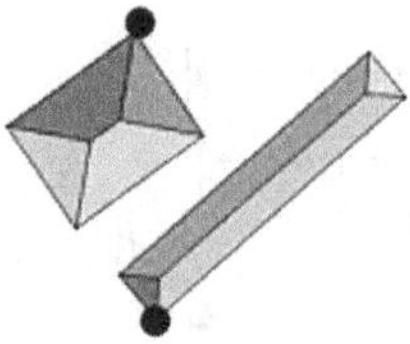

D.

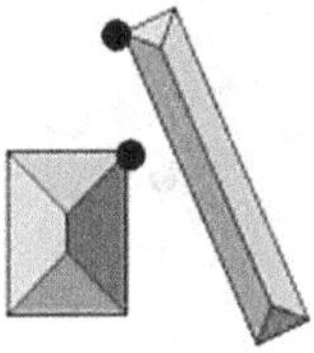

Answer

ANSWERS TO SPATIAL REASONING TEST EXERCISE 2

1. B
2. C
3. C
4. C
5. A
6. B
7. B
8. C

MECHANICAL COMPREHENSION TEST

Mechanical comprehension tests are an assessment that measures an individual's aptitude to learn mechanical skills. The tests are usually multiple choice in nature and present simple, frequently encountered mechanisms and situations. The majority of mechanical comprehension tests require a working knowledge of basic mechanical operations and the application of physical laws. On the following pages I have provided you with a number of example questions to help you prepare for the tests. Work through them as quickly as possible but remember to go back and check which ones you get wrong; more importantly, make sure you understand how the correct answer is reached.

In this particular exercise there are 20 questions and you have 10 minutes in which to answer them.

Question 1

If Circle 'B' turns in a Clockwise direction, which way will circle 'A' turn?

A. Clockwise

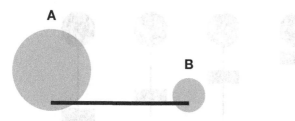

B. Anti-Clockwise

C. Backwards and forwards

D. It won't move

Answer

Question 2

Which square is carrying the heaviest load?

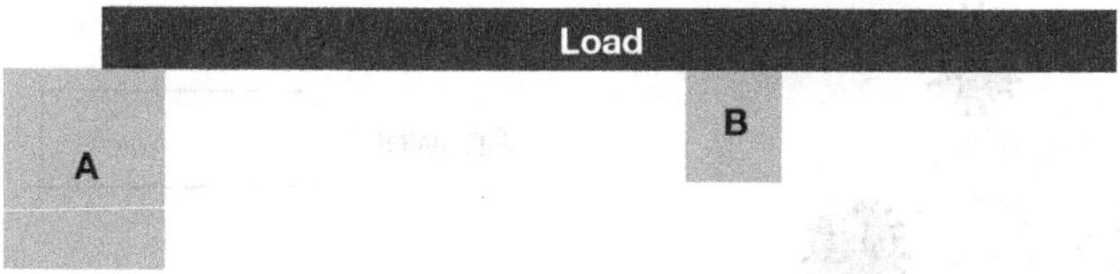

A. Square A

B. Square B

Answer

Question 3

Which pendulum will swing at the slowest speed?

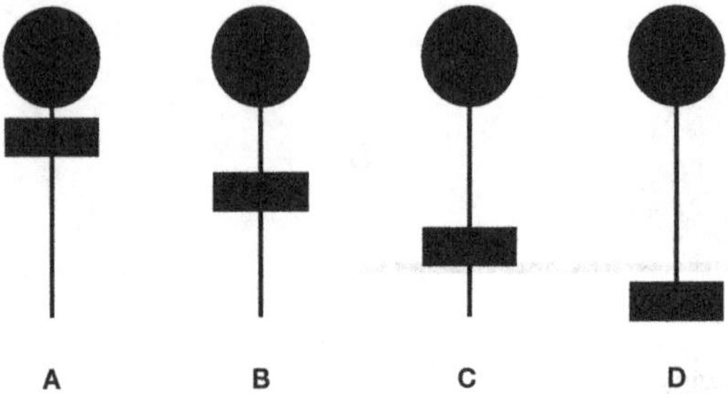

Answer

Question 4

If Cog 'A' turns in an anti-clockwise direction which way will Cog 'B' turn?

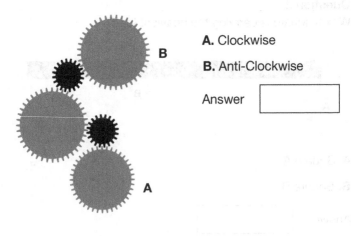

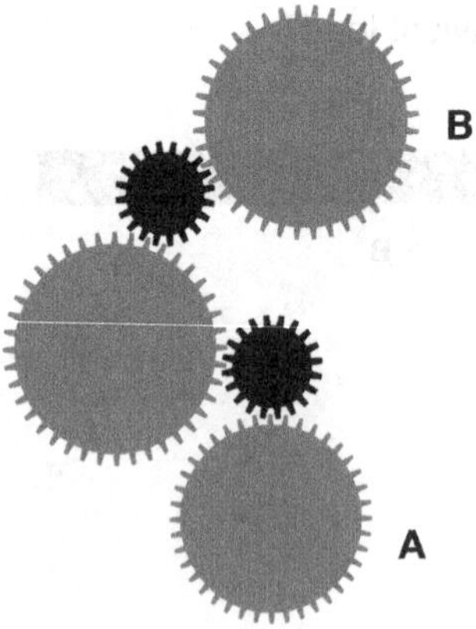

A. Clockwise

B. Anti-Clockwise

Answer

Question 5

If Cog 'B' moves in a clockwise direction, which way will Cog 'A' turn?

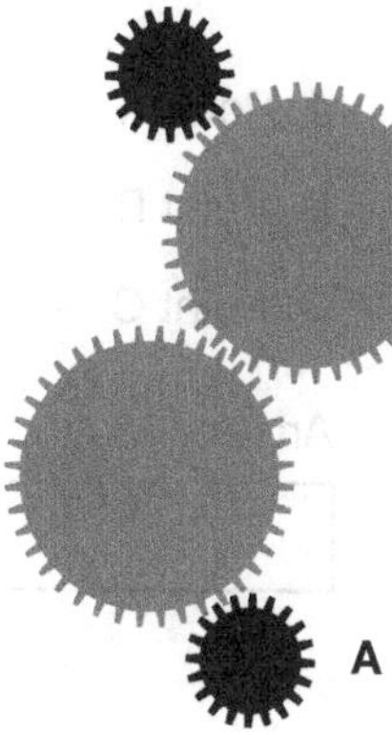

A. Clockwise

B. Anti-Clockwise

Answer

Question 6

Which shelf can carry the greatest load?

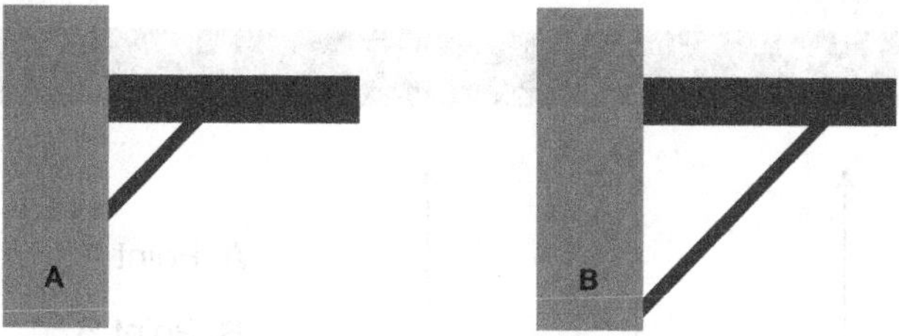

A. Shelf A

B. Shelf B

Answer

Question 7

At which point will the pendulum be travelling at the greatest speed?

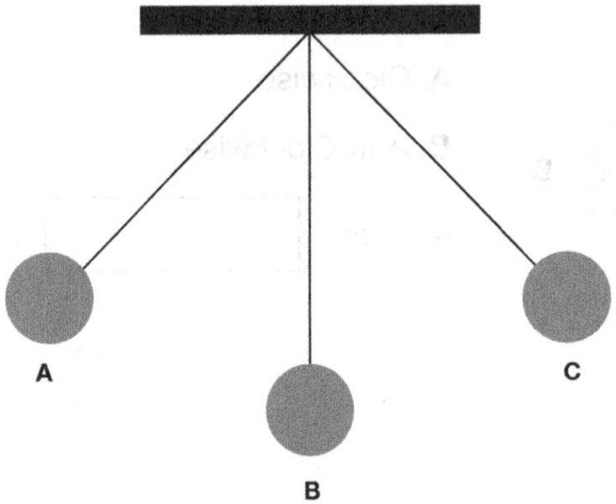

A. Point A

B. Point B

C. Point C

Answer

Question 8

At which point will the beam balance?

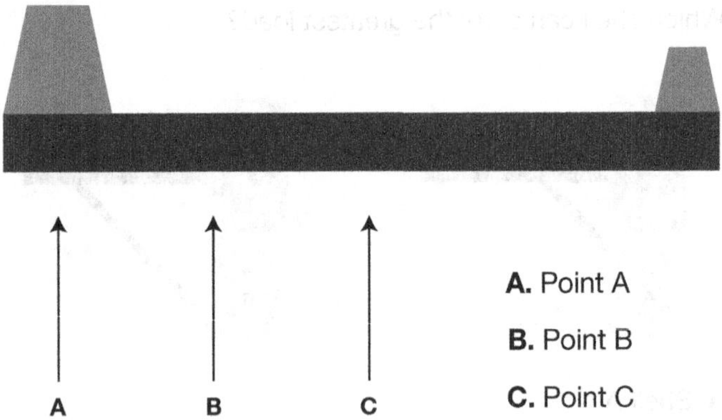

A. Point A

B. Point B

C. Point C

Answer

Question 9

If water is poured into the narrow tube, up to point 'X', what height would it reach in the wide tube?

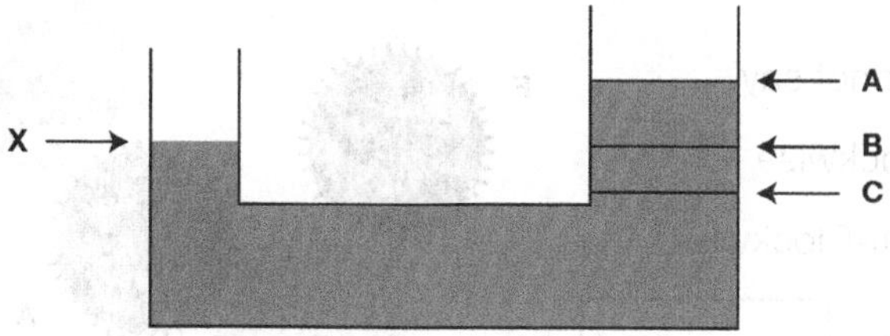

A. Point A

B. Point B

C. Point C

Answer

Question 10

At which point would Ball 'Y' have to be at to balance out Ball 'X'?

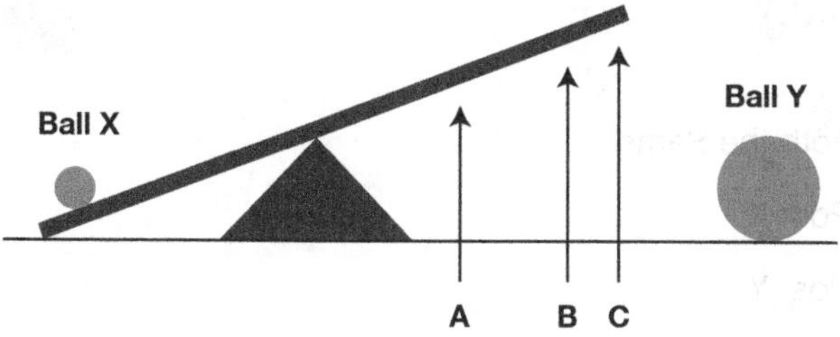

A. Point A

B. Point B

C. Point C

Answer

Question 11

If Cog 'A' turns anti-clockwise, which way will Cog 'F' turn?

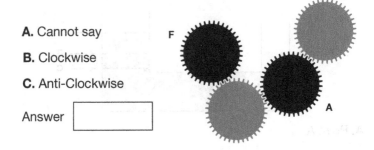

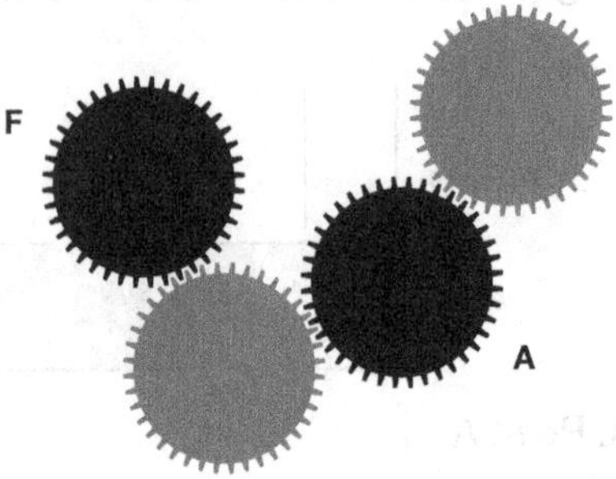

A. Cannot say

B. Clockwise

C. Anti-Clockwise

Answer

Question 12

Which post is carrying the heaviest load?

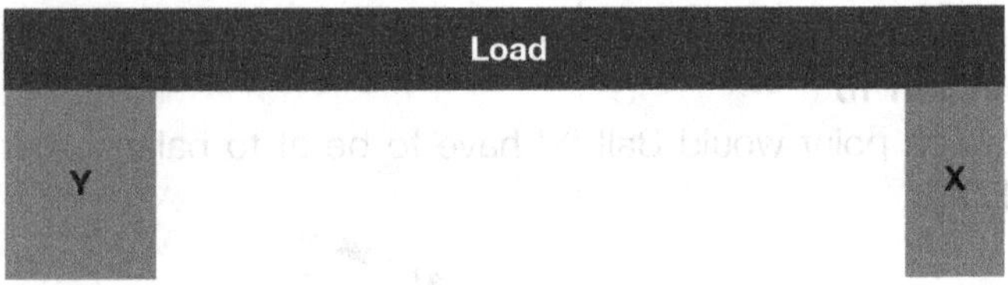

A. Both the Same

B. Post X

C. Post Y

Answer

Question 13

If water is poured in at Point D, which tube will overflow first?

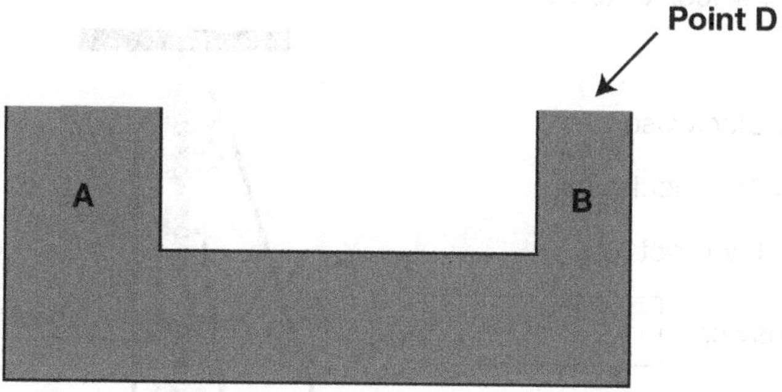

A. Tube A

B. Both the same

C. Tube B

Answer

Question 14

At which point would it be easier to haul up load X?

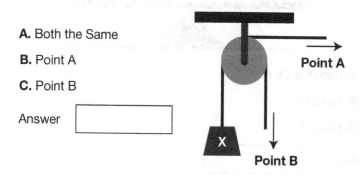

A. Both the Same

B. Point A

C. Point B

Answer

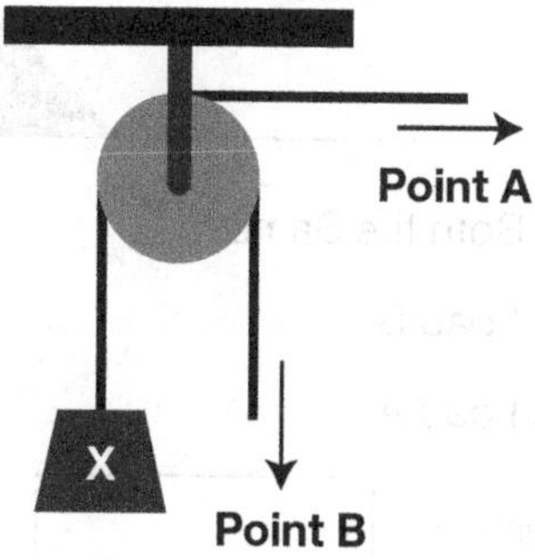

Question 15

If rope 'A' is pulled in the direction of the arrow, which way will wheel 'C' turn?

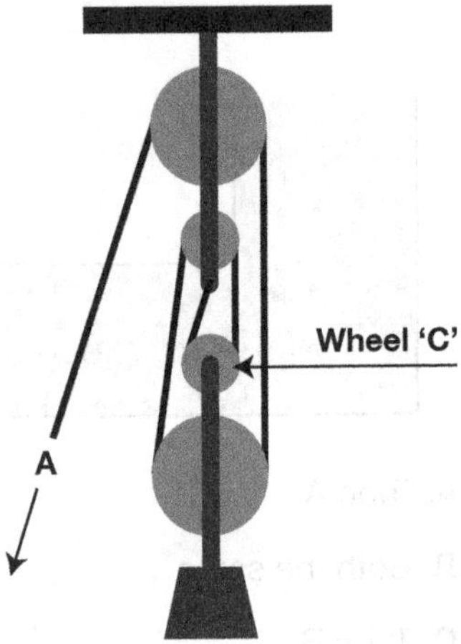

A. Clockwise

B. Anti-clockwise

C. It will not turn

Answer

Question 16

Which load is the heaviest?

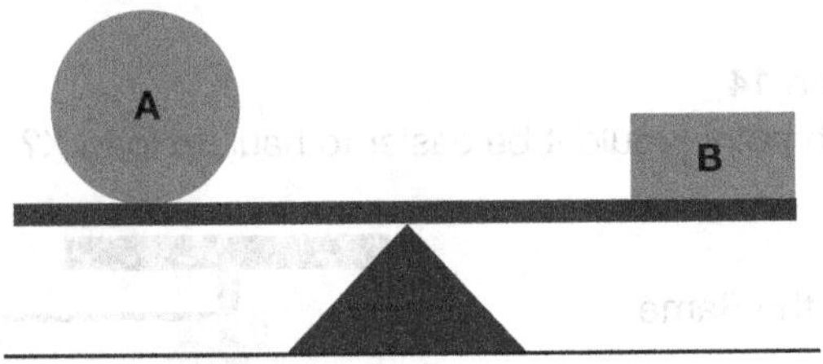

A. Both the Same

B. Load B

C. Load A

Answer

Question 17

If rope 'A' is pulled in the direction of the arrow, which direction will Load 'Q' travel in?

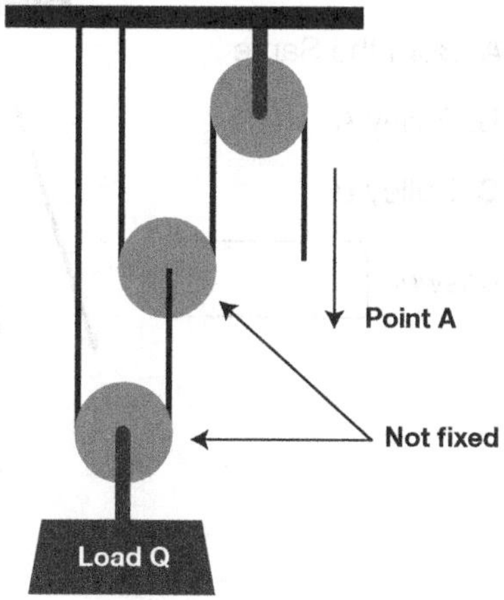

A. It will not move

B. Down

C. Up

Answer

Question 18

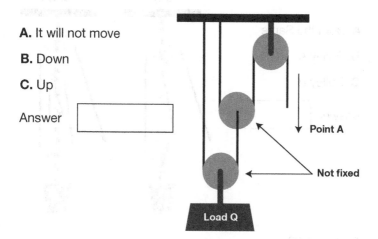

If circle 'X' turns anti-clockwise, which way will circle 'Y' turn?

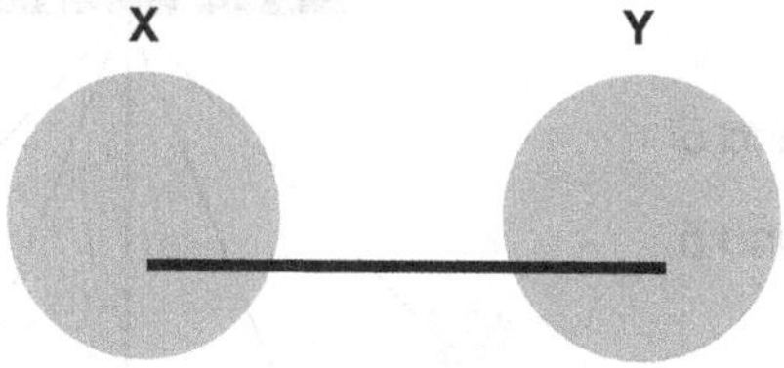

A. Anti-clockwise

B. Clockwise

C. Backwards and forwards

Answer

Question 19

Which pulley system will be the easiest to lift the bucket of water?

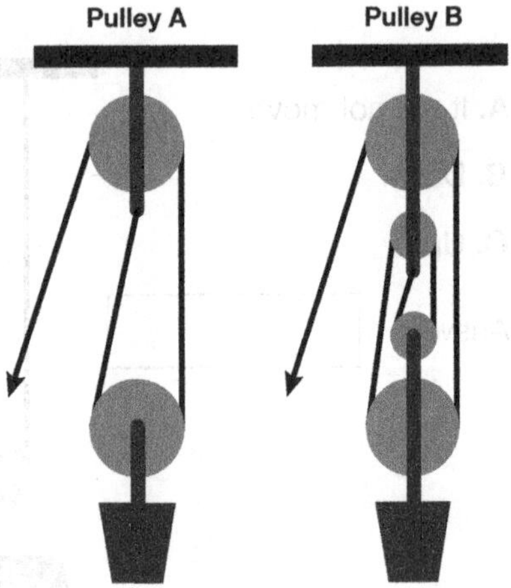

A. Both the Same

B. Pulley A

C. Pulley B

Answer

Question 20

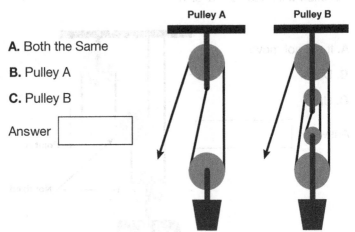

At which point(s) will the pendulum be swinging the fastest?

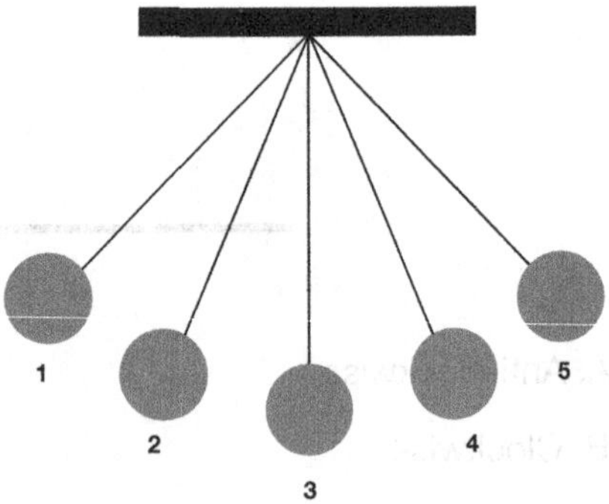

A. Point 1

B. Points 1 and 5

C. Points 3 and 5

D. Point 3

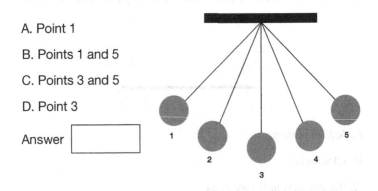

Answer

ANSWERS TO MECHANICAL COMPREHENSION TEST

1. C
2. B
3. D
4. B
5. A
6. B
7. B
8. B
9. B
10. A
11. C
12. C
13. B
14. A
15. B
16. A
17. C
18. A
19. C
20. D

ELECTRICAL COMPREHENSION TEST

During the AST you will be required to sit an Electrical Comprehension Test. The test itself is designed to assess your ability to work with different electrical concepts. On the following pages I have provided you with a number of sample questions to help you prepare for the tests. Work through them as quickly as possible but remember to go back and check the questions you may have got wrong and, more importantly, make sure you understand the correct answers. If you struggle to understand the concepts of electrical circuits and terminology then you may wish to purchase a booklet which will help you to understand how they work. You will be able to obtain a book from all good bookstores including www.amazon.co.uk.

In this particular exercise you have 10 minutes in which to answer the 22 questions.

ELECTRICAL COMPREHENSION TEST EXERCISE 1

Question 1

Electrical power is measured in what?

A. Watts **B.** Amps **C.** Volts **D.** Centimetres

Answer

Question 2

The basic particles that make up an atom are what?

A. Neutrons, protons and electrons

B. Protons, neutrons and particles

C. Protons and electrons

D. Mesons, neutrons and electrons

Answer

Question 3

Which of the following statements best describes Ohm's Law?

A. The relationship between voltage, current and resistance, expressed by the equation V=IR, where V is the voltage in volts, I is the current in amperes, and R is the resistance in ohms.

B. The total resistance in an electrical circuit.

C. $E = MC^2$.

D. An equation.

Question 4
10 kilovolts is the equivalent to which of the following?

A. 10 millivolts

B. 1.0 volts

C. 1000 volts

D. 10000 volts

Answer

Question 5
Ohm's Law states that current is directly proportional to which of the following?

A. Resistance

B. Voltage

C. Temperature

D. Gas

Answer

Question 6
The unit of electrical potential or pressure is which of the following?

A. Watt

B. Amp

C. Volt

D. Current

Answer

Question 7
Removing the electrons from an atom would make the atom what?

A. Positively charged

B. Neutral

C. Negatively charged

D. A positive ion

Answer

Question 8
Current is measured in what?

A. Volts

B. Amps

C. Ohms

D. Watts

Answer

Question 9
Resistance is measured in what?

A. Volts

B. Amps

C. Ohms

D. Watts

Answer

Question 10
The ampere is a measure of what?

A. The power in a circuit.

B. The number of amps across a resistor.

C. The electrical pressure flowing in a circuit.

D. The number of electrons per second flowing in a circuit past a given point.

Answer

Question 11
What is the SI unit of capacitance?

A. Ohm

B. Farad

C. Watt

D. Amps

Answer

Question 12
Which of the following is NOT an effect of an electrical current?

A. Chemical

B. Sound

C. Heat

D. Light

Answer

Question 13

In the following circuit, what happens if the switch remains open?

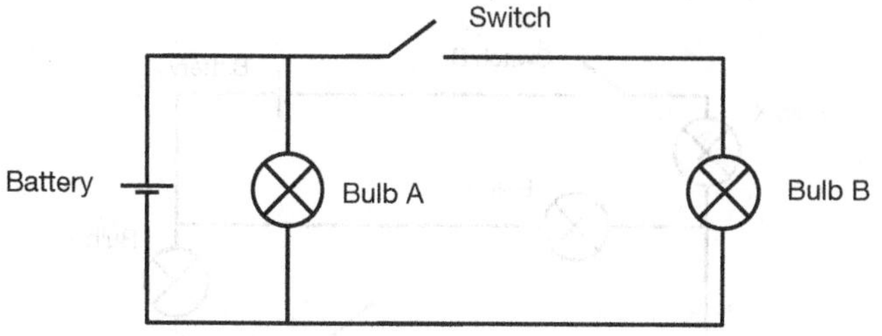

A. Bulbs A and B will illuminate.

B. Bulb B will illuminate only.

C. Bulb A will illuminate only.

D. No bulbs will illuminate.

Answer

Question 14

In the following circuit, if switch A closes and switch B remains open, what will happen?

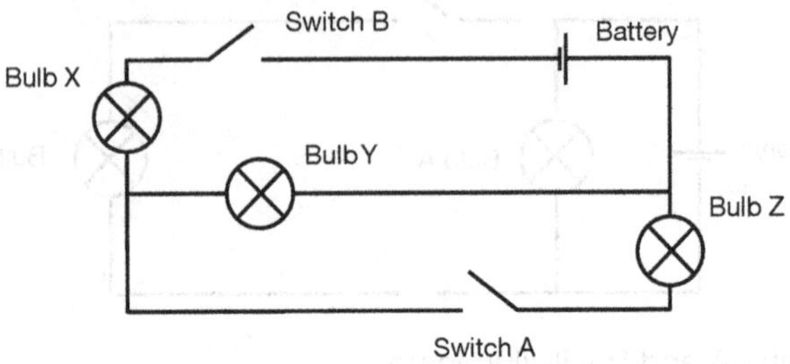

A. Bulbs X, Y, and Z will illuminate.

B. Bulb X will illuminate only.

C. Bulbs Y and Z will illuminate only.

D. No bulbs will illuminate.

Answer

Question 15

What will be the voltage at Point A if the battery is 12 Volts and the bulbs are of the same type?

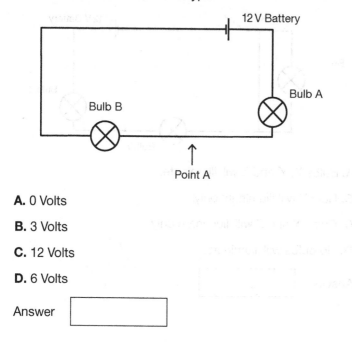

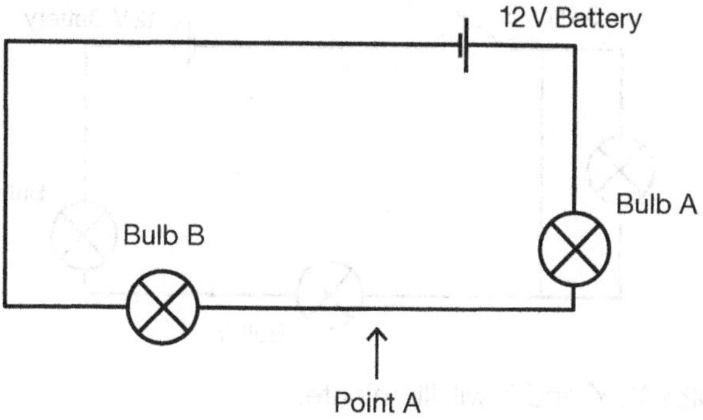

A. 0 Volts

B. 3 Volts

C. 12 Volts

D. 6 Volts

Answer

Question 16

If switch B remains open, what will happen?

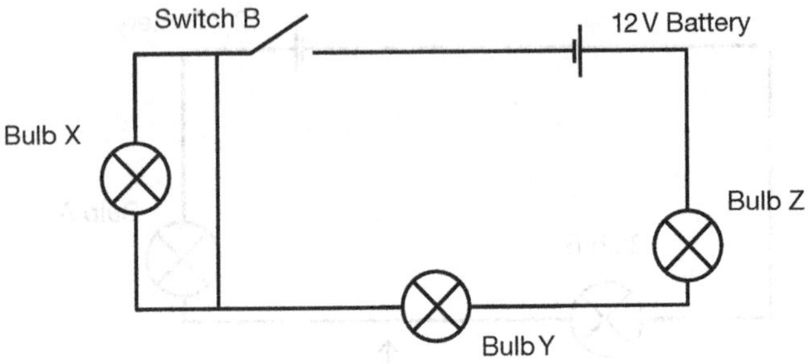

A. Bulbs X, Y, and Z will illuminate.

B. Bulb X will illuminate only.

C. Bulbs Y and Z will illuminate only.

D. No bulbs will illuminate.

Answer

Question 17

In the following electrical circuit, if switch A closes and switch B and switch C remain open, what will happen?

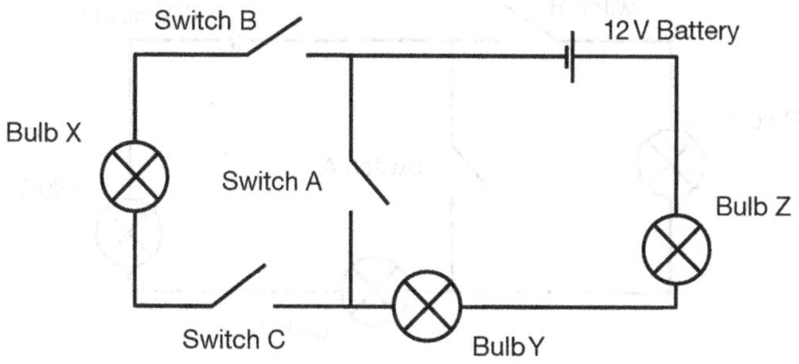

A. Bulbs X, Y, and Z will illuminate.

B. Bulb X will illuminate only.

C. Bulbs Y and Z will illuminate only.

D. No bulbs will illuminate.

Answer

Question 18

In the following electrical circuit, if switch A remains open and switch B closes, what will happen?

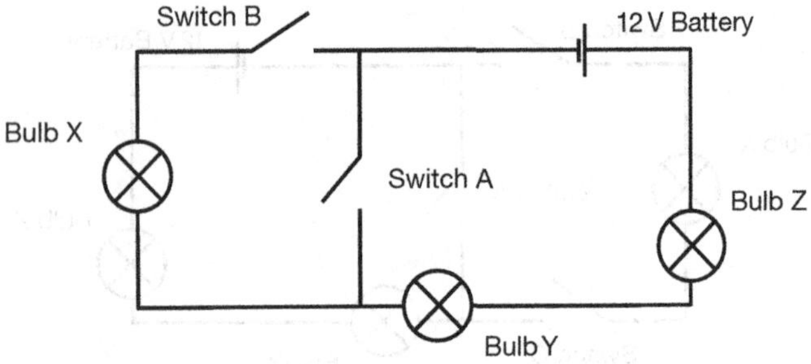

A. Bulbs X, Y, and Z will illuminate.

B. Bulb Xwill illuminate only.

C. Bulbs Y and Z will illuminate only.

D. No bulbs will illuminate.

Answer

Question 19

In the following circuit, with switch A open, which bulbs are illuminated (if any)?

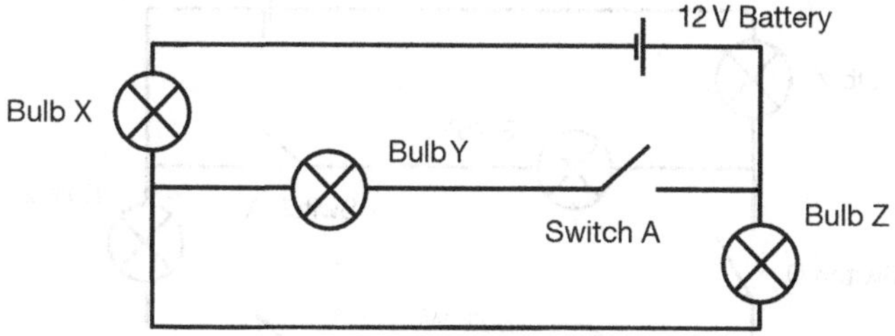

A. Bulbs X, Y, and Z will illuminate.

B. Bulb Y will illuminate only.

C. Bulbs × and Z will illuminate only.

D. No bulbs will illuminate.

Answer

Question 20

In the following circuit, if switch A closes, what will happen?

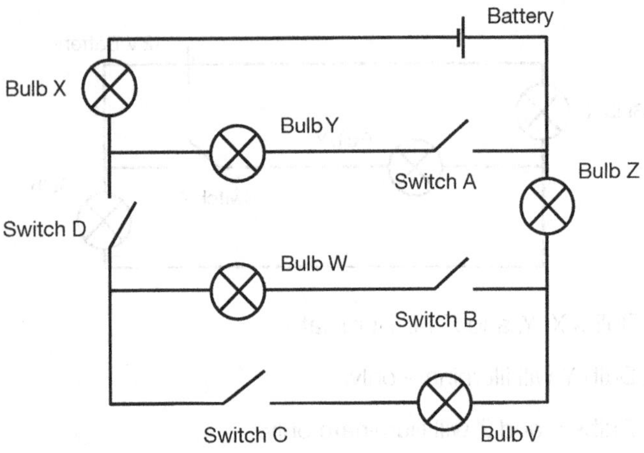

A. Bulbs V, W, X, Y, and Z will illuminate.

B. Bulb Xand Y will illuminate only.

C. Bulbs X, Y and Z will illuminate only.

D. No bulbs will illuminate.

Answer

Question 21

In the following circuit, if switch A and switch B remain open and switches C and D close, what will happen?

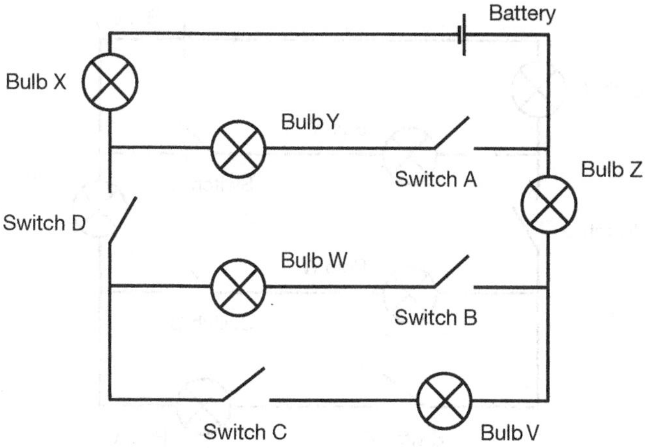

A. Bulbs V, W, X, Y, and Z will illuminate.

B. Bulb V, X, Z and Y will illuminate only.

C. Bulbs V, × and Z will illuminate only.

D. No bulbs will illuminate.

Answer

Question 22

In the following circuit, if switch A and switch D remain open and switches B and C close, what will happen?

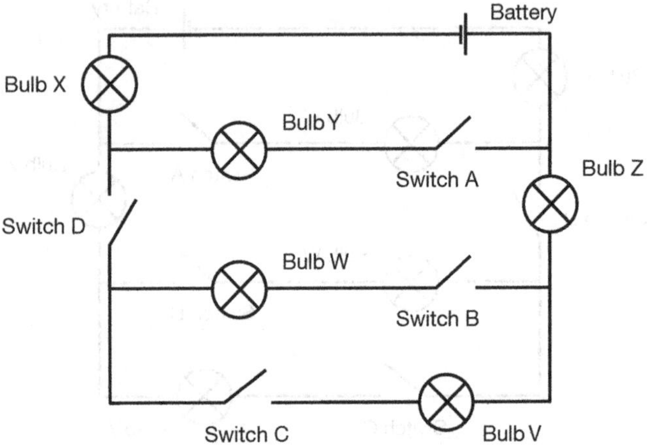

A. Bulbs V, W, will illuminate.

B. Bulb V, W, X, Y and Z will illuminate.

C. Bulbs V, W and Z will illuminate only.

D. No bulbs will illuminate.

Answer

ANSWERS TO ELECTRICAL COMPREHENSION EXERCISE

1. A
2. A
3. A
4. D
5. A
6. C
7. D
8. B
9. C
10. D
11. B
12. B
13. C
14. D
15. C
16. D
17. C
18. A
19. C
20. B
21. C
22. D

MEMORY TEST

During the Airman/Airwoman selection test you will be required to undertake a memory test. The test is usually in two parts. During the first part of the test you will be required to view a sequence of letters. The letters will appear on a screen for a period of time. After a period of time the sequence will disappear and you will then be required to answer questions relating to that sequence.

Let's assume that the sequence of letters looks like the following. Please note that during the real test the letters may appear individually over a set period of time and not collectively as per below.

W	**E**	**Q**	**X**	**R**	**E**

Study the above sequence of letters for one minute only. Once the minute is up, cover the above sequence with your hand or a sheet of paper, and answer the following questions:

Question 1

How many letter E's were in the sequence?

Answer

Question 2

How many letters were there in between the letter W and the letter X?

Answer

Question 3

What letter was between the letter Q and the letter R?

Answer

Hopefully you managed to get the questions correct. Your ability to successfully pass this test will be dependant on how good your memory is. In order to improve your ability during this test try the following sample exercise.

MEMORY TEST EXERCISE 1

R	A	L	E	S	S

Study the above sequence of letters for one minute only. Once the minute is up, cover the above sequence with your hand or a sheet of paper, and answer the following questions:

Question 1

How many letter S's were in the sequence?

Answer

Question 2

How many letters were there in between the letter R and the letter E?

Answer

Question 3

What was the first letter in the sequence?

Answer

MEMORY TEST EXERCISE 2

F	A	Q	A	Q	S

Study the above sequence of letters for one minute only. Once the minute is up, cover the above sequence with your hand or a sheet of paper, and answer the following questions:

Question 1
How many letters were there in the entire sequence?

Answer

Question 2
How many letters were there in between the letter F and the letter S?

Answer

Question 3
What was the third letter in the sequence?

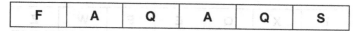

Answer

MEMORY TEST EXERCISE 3

E	X	Q	E	E	W	Z

Study the above sequence of letters for one minute only. Once the minute is up, cover the above sequence with your hand or a sheet of paper, and answer the following questions:

Question 1
How many letters were there in the entire sequence?

Answer

Question 2
How many letter E's were there in the sequence?

Answer

Question 3
How many letters were there in between the letter Q and the letter W?

Answer

MEMORY TEST EXERCISE 4

Y	t	d	D	w	W	g

Study the above sequence of letters for one minute only. Once the minute is up, cover the above sequence with your hand or a sheet of paper, and answer the following questions:

Question 1

How many capital letters were there in the sequence?

Answer

Question 2

How many lower case (non capital) letters were there in the sequence?

Answer

Question 3

How many letters were there in between the letter t and the letter g?

Answer

MEMORY TEST EXERCISE 5

S	k	T	t	Y	U	T	t

Study the above sequence of letters for one minute only. Once the minute is up, cover the above sequence with your hand or a sheet of paper, and answer the following questions:

Question 1

How many capital letters were there in the sequence?

Answer

Question 2

How many letters were there in the entire sequence?

Answer

Question 3

How many capital letters were there in between the letter k and the letter U?

Answer

MEMORY TEST EXERCISE 6

x	c	o	y	L	t	G	g

Study the above sequence of letters for one minute only. Once the minute is up, cover the above sequence with your hand or a sheet of paper, and answer the following questions:

Question 1

How many lower case (non capital) letters were there in the sequence?

Answer

Question 2

How many letters were there between the letter x and the letter G?

Answer

Question 3

How many lower case (non capital) letters were there in between the letter x and the letter G?

Answer

MEMORY TEST EXERCISE 7

p	y	T	t	R

Study the above sequence of letters for one minute only. Once the minute is up, cover the above sequence with your hand or a sheet of paper, and answer the following questions:

Question 1

How many capital letters were there in the sequence?

Answer

Question 2

How many capital letters were there between the letter y and the letter R?

Answer

Question 3

What was the fourth letter in the sequence?

Answer

MEMORY TEST EXERCISE 8

O	Q	s	S	A	a	G

Study the above sequence of letters for one minute only. Once the minute is up, cover the above sequence with your hand or a sheet of paper, and answer the following questions:

Question 1

How many capital letters were there in the sequence?

Answer

Question 2

What were the fifth and sixth letters in the sequence?

Answer

Question 3

What was the last letter in the sequence?

Answer

MEMORY TEST EXERCISE 9

t	t	r	S	W	t	Q

Study the above sequence of letters for one minute only. Once the minute is up, cover the above sequence with your hand or a sheet of paper, and answer the following questions:

Question 1
Which letter appears the most times in the sequence?

Answer

Question 2
What was the fifth letter in the sequence?

Answer

Question 3
Which two letters appear between the letter S and the letter Q?

Answer

MEMORY TEST EXERCISE 10

v	b	n	q	w	A	s	s	d

Study the above sequence of letters for one minute only. Once the minute is up, cover the above sequence with your hand or a sheet of paper, and answer the following questions:

Question 1
How many letters were there in the sequence?

Answer

Question 2
What was the third letter in the sequence?

Answer

Question 3
Which letter appears the most in the sequence?

Answer

ANSWERS TO MEMORY TEST EXERCISES

Memory test exercise 1

1. 2
2. 2
3. R

Memory test exercise 2

1. 6
2. 4
3. Q

Memory test exercise 3

1. 7
2. 3
3. 2

Memory test exercise 4

1. 3
2. 4
3. 4

Memory test exercise 5

1. 5
2. 8
3. 2

Memory test exercise 6

1. 6
2. 5
3. 4

Memory test exercise 7

1. 2
2. 1
3. t

Memory test exercise 8

1. 5
2. A + a
3. G

Memory test exercise 9

1. t
2. W
3. W + t

Memory test exercise 10

1. 9
2. n
3. s

MEMORY TEST PART 2

During the second part of the test you will be required to view a number of different grids which contain coloured squares. Each grid will appear individually. Once the sequence of grids has disappeared you will be required to state which pattern the collective coloured squares make up from a number of different options.

Take a look at the following four grids. Please note: during the real test each grid will only appear one at a time and for a brief period of time. You will need to memorise the position of the coloured squares in each grid in order to answer the question.

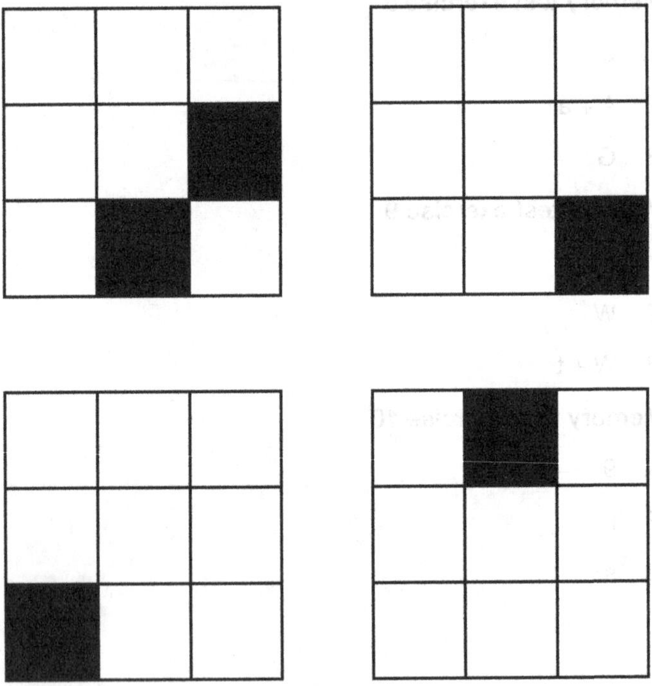

Once you have studied the grids cover them with your hand or a sheet of paper. Now decide from the following four options which grid contains the collective group of coloured squares from the four grids.

Option 1

Option 2

Option 3

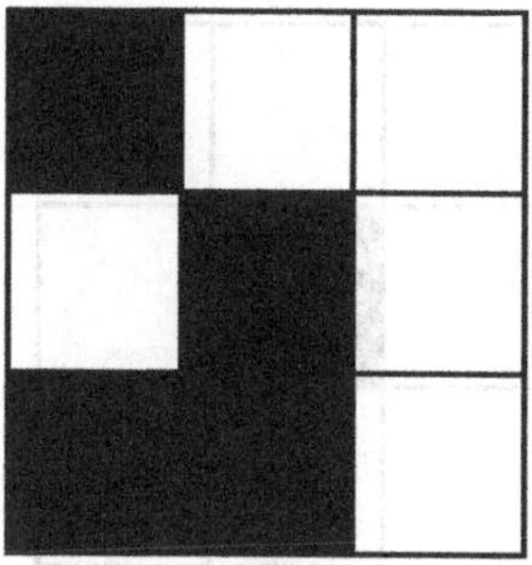

Option 4

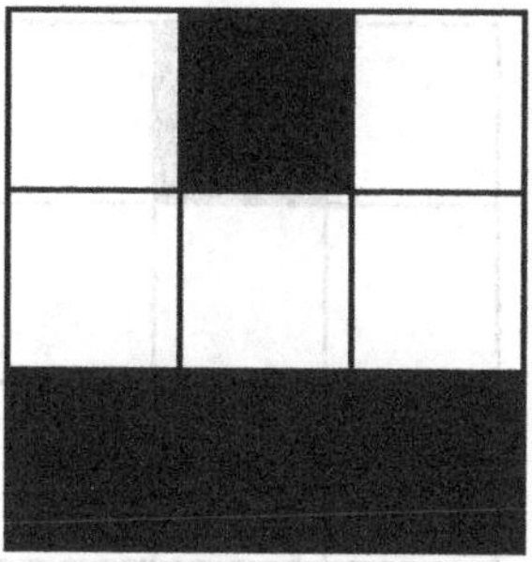

As you will see, Option 1 accurately reflects the combined locations of the coloured squares from the initial four grids.

Once you understand what is required, move on to the following exercises.

QUESTION 1

Study the following grids for 10 seconds only. Then turn the page and decide from the four options available which grid contains the collective group of coloured squares from the grids.

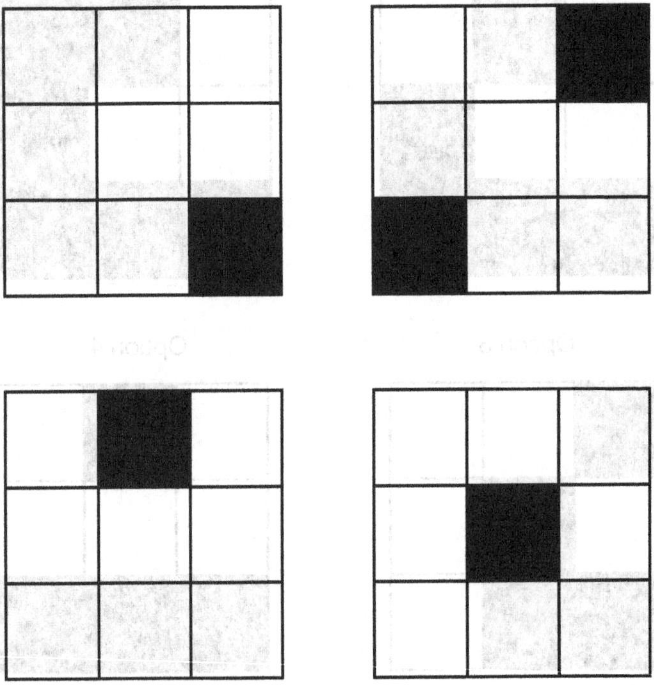

QUESTION 1 OPTIONS

Option 1

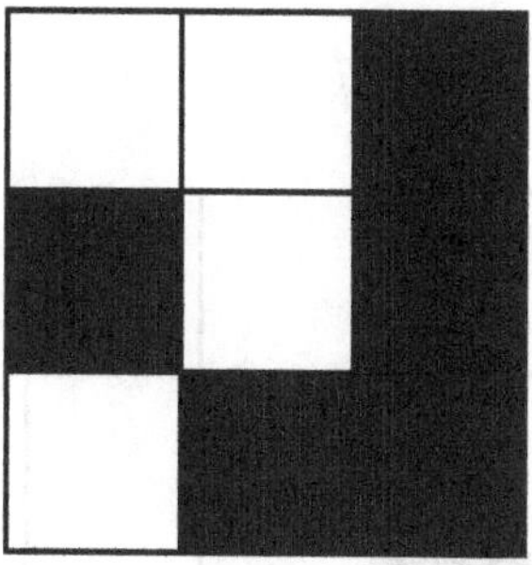

Option 2

Option 3

Option 4

Answer

QUESTION 2

Study the following grids for 10 seconds only. Then turn the page and decide from the four options available which grid contains the collective group of coloured squares from the grids.

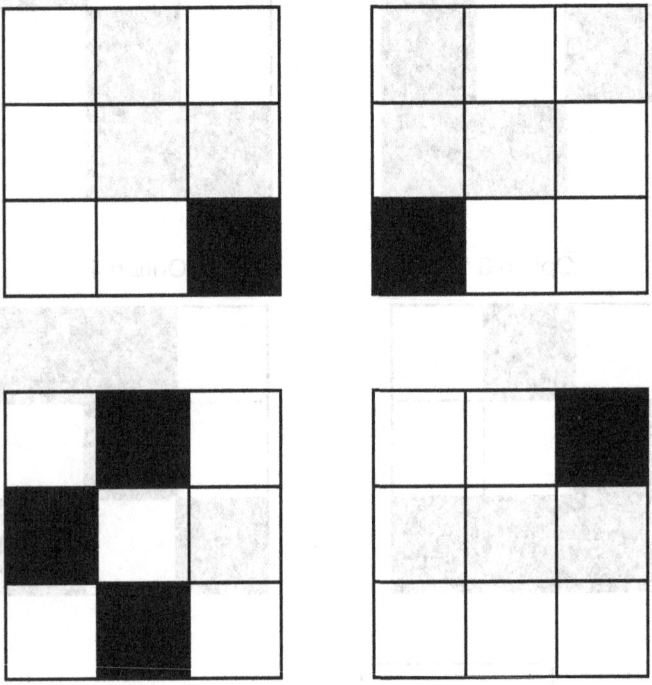

QUESTION 2 OPTIONS

Option 1

Option 2

Option 3

Option 4

Answer

QUESTION 3

Study the following grids for 10 seconds only. Then turn the page and decide from the four options available which grid contains the collective group of coloured squares from the grids.

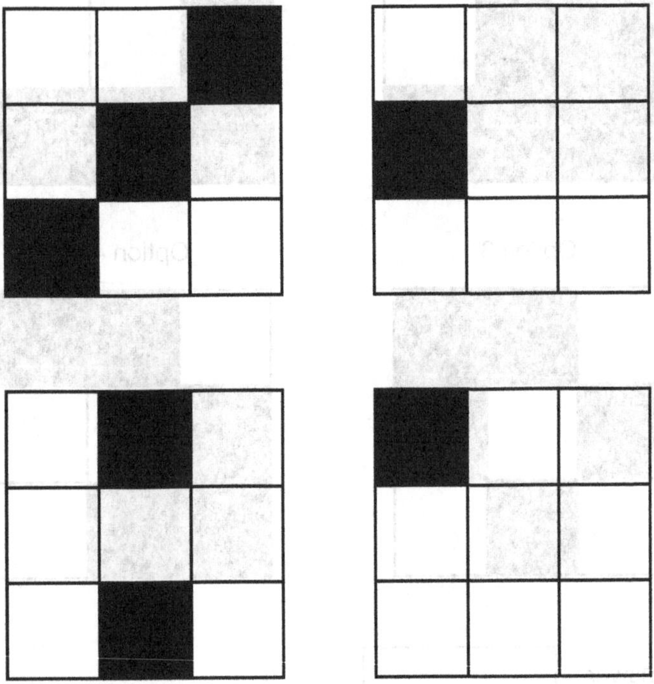

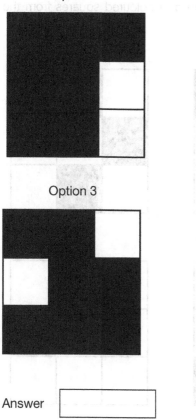

QUESTION 3 OPTIONS

Option 1

Option 2

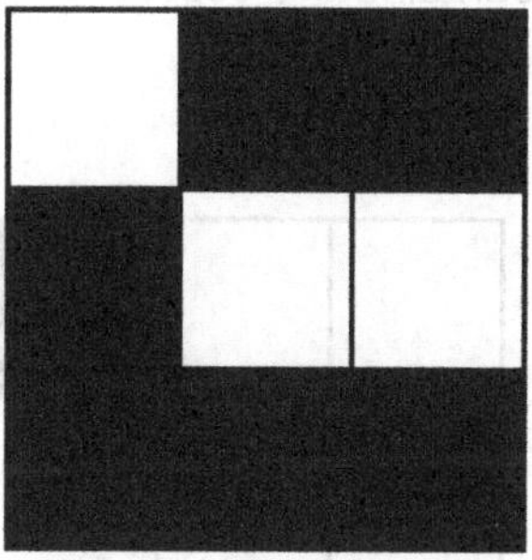

Option 3

Option 4

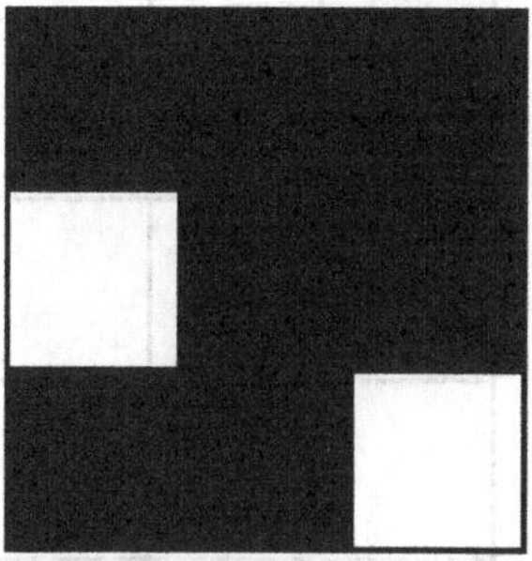

Answer

QUESTION 4

Study the following grids for 10 seconds only. Then turn the page and decide from the four options available which grid contains the collective group of coloured squares from the grids.

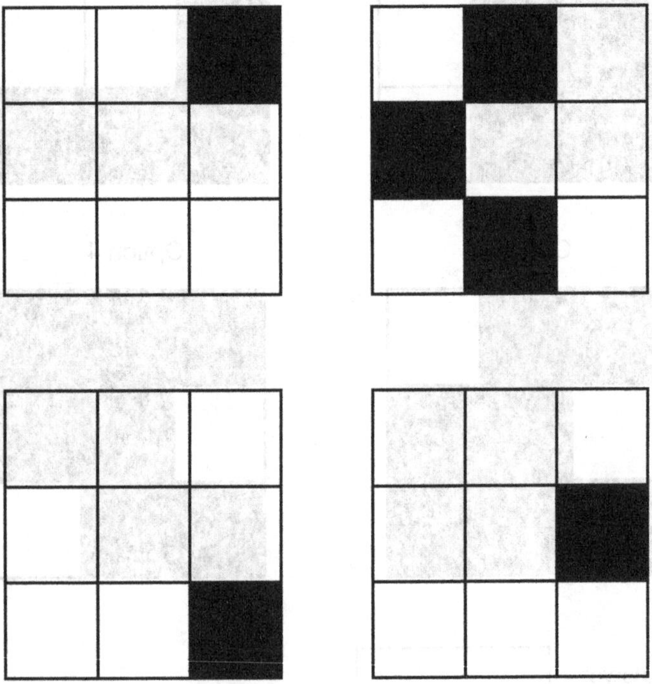

QUESTION 4 OPTIONS

Option 1

Option 2

Option 3

Option 4

Answer

QUESTION 5

Study the following grids for 10 seconds only. Then turn the page and decide from the four options available which grid contains the collective group of coloured squares from the grids.

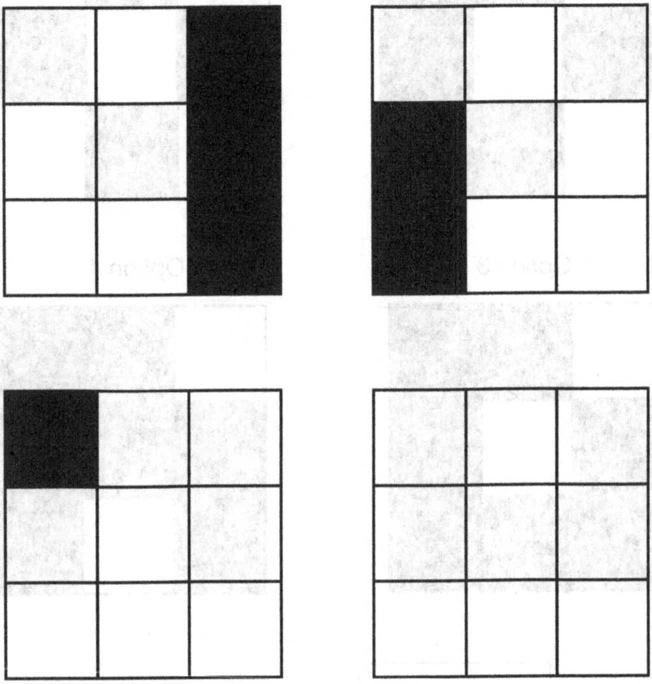

QUESTION 5 OPTIONS

Option 1

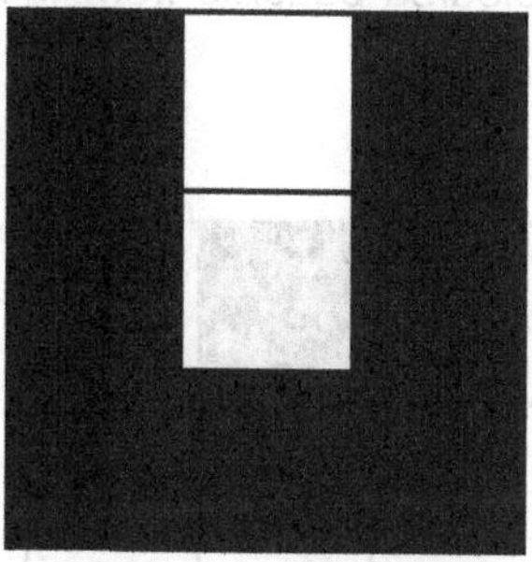

Option 2

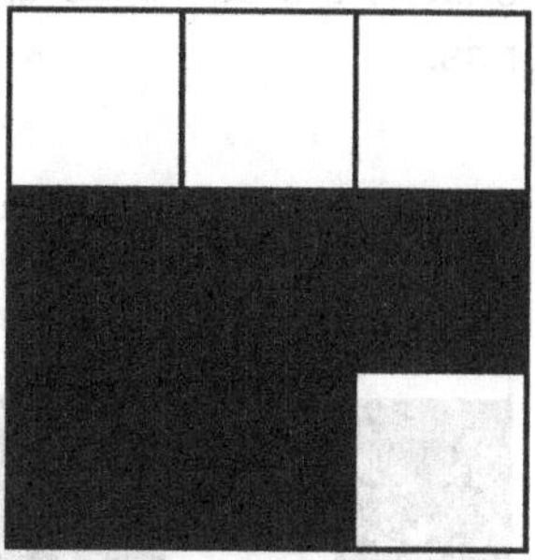

Option 3

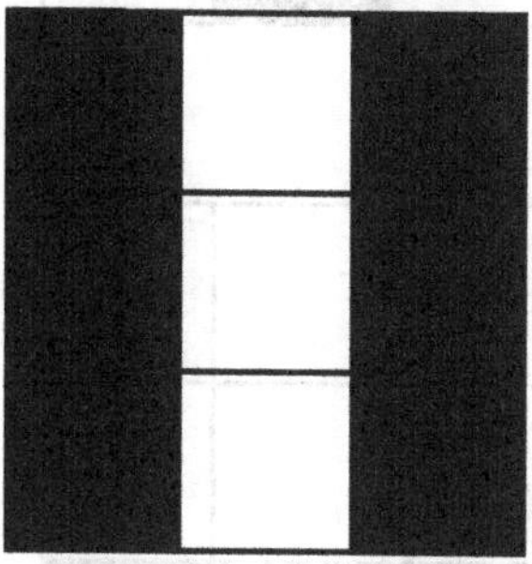

Option 4

Answer

QUESTION 6

Study the following grids for 10 seconds only. Then turn the page and decide from the four options available which grid contains the collective group of coloured squares from the grids.

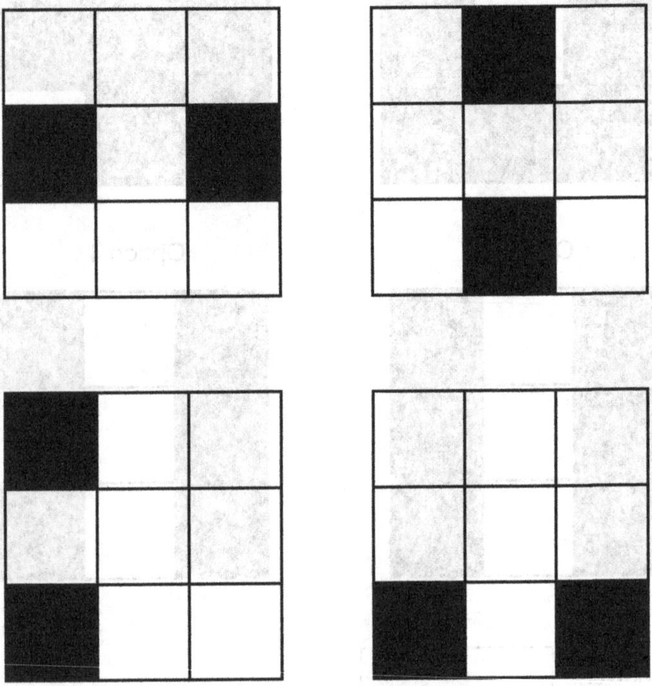

QUESTION 6 OPTIONS

Option 1

Option 2

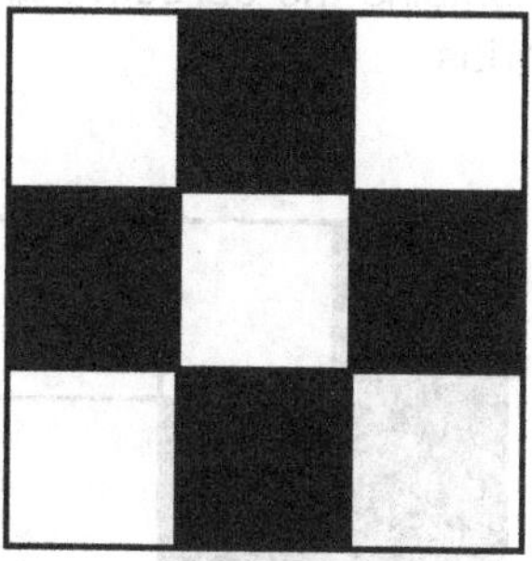

Option 3

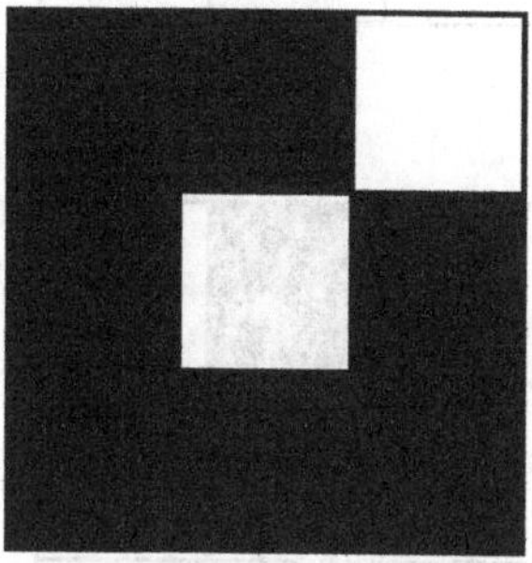

Option 4

Answer

QUESTION 7

Study the following grids for 10 seconds only. Then turn the page and decide from the four options available which grid contains the collective group of coloured squares from the grids.

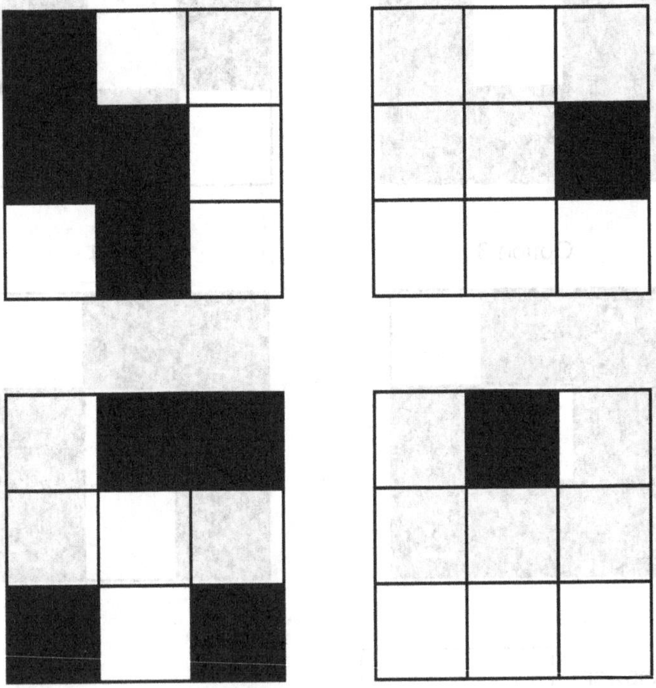

QUESTION 7 OPTIONS

Option 1

Option 2

Option 3

Option 4

Answer

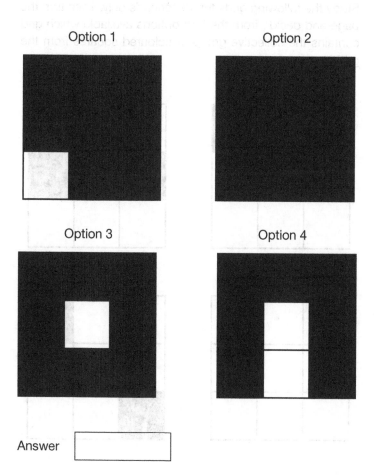

QUESTION 8

Study the following grids for 10 seconds only. Then turn the page and decide from the four options available which grid contains the collective group of coloured squares from the grids.

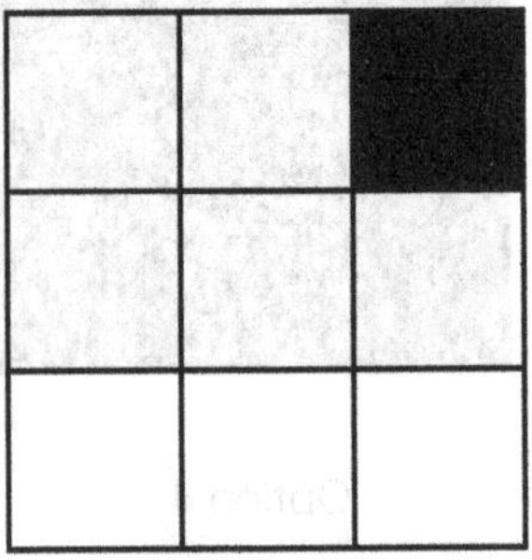

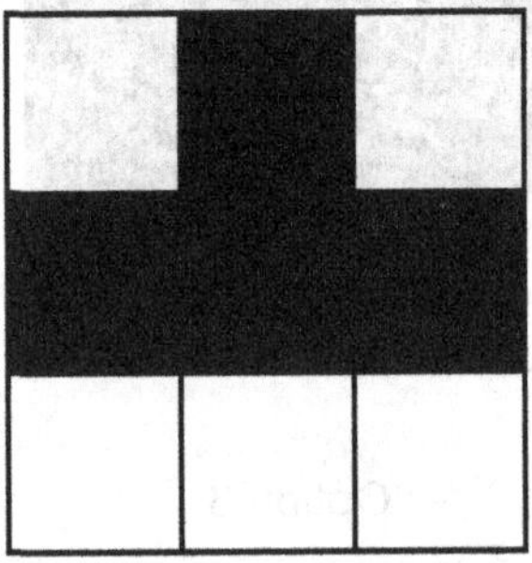

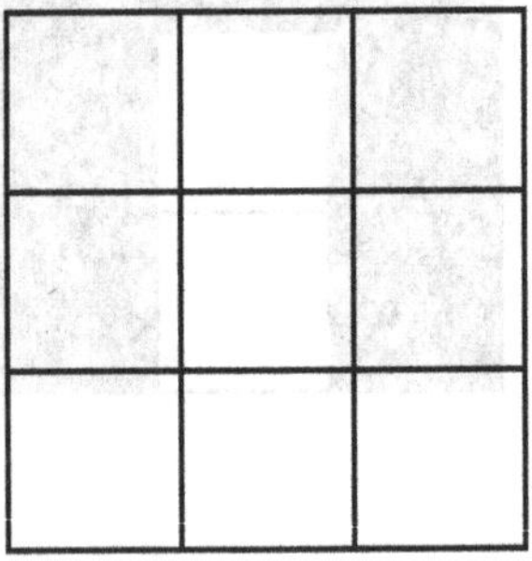

QUESTION 8 OPTIONS

Option 1

Option 2

Option 3

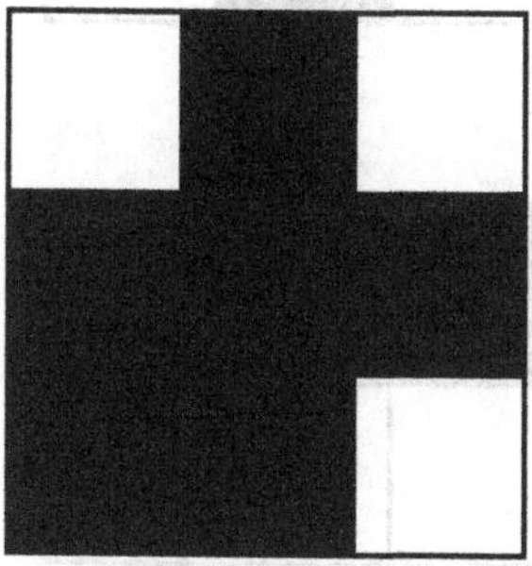

Option 4

Answer

QUESTION 9

Study the following grids for 10 seconds only. Then turn the page and decide from the four options available which grid contains the collective group of coloured squares from the grids.

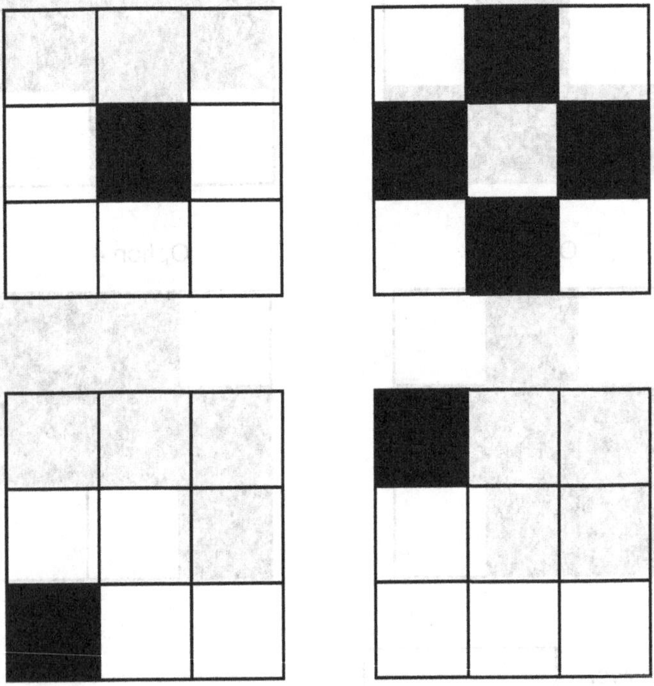

QUESTION 9 OPTIONS

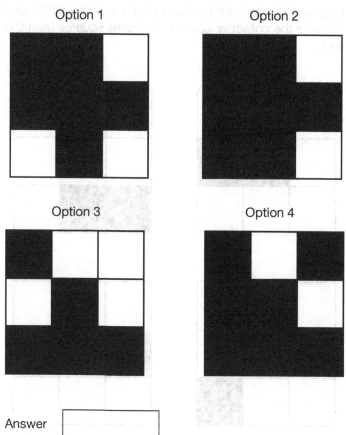

Option 1

Option 2

Option 3

Option 4

Answer

QUESTION 10

Study the following grids for 10 seconds only. Then turn the page and decide from the four options available which grid contains the collective group of coloured squares from the grids.

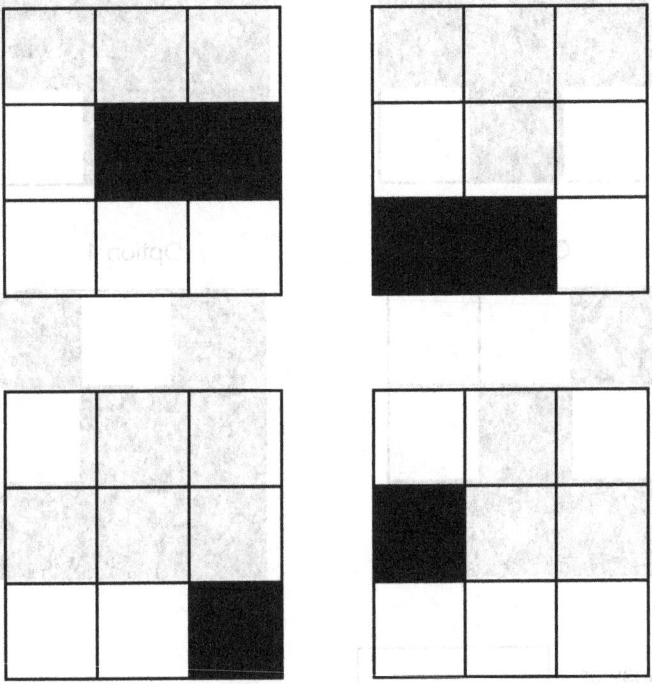

QUESTION 10 OPTIONS

Option 1

Option 2

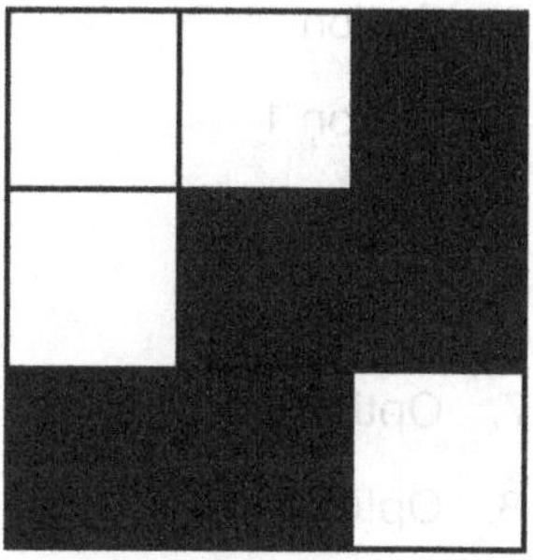

Option 3

Option 4

Answer

ANSWERS TO MEMORY TEST PART 2

1. Option 4
2. Option 2
3. Option 1
4. Option 1
5. Option 3
6. Option 3
7. Option 2
8. Option 4
9. Option 2
10. Option 1

FINAL TIPS FOR PASSING THE AIRMAN/AIRWOMAN SELECTION TEST

- Your ability to successfully pass the AST is purely dependant on the amount of practice you put in during the build up to your test. Don't leave it until the night before your test to start practising. Build into your action plan now the times and dates that you intend to improve your ability in this area.
- Practice little and often. You will see a far greater improvement if you practice 20 minutes everyday as opposed to 2 hours one day a week.
- Consider obtaining more testing books to help you prepare. Remember, the more tests you do the better you will become.
- Check every incorrect answer to see where you went wrong. This is crucial in your development.
- Practice without a calculator and practice under timed conditions.

CHAPTER SIX

THE RAF INTERVIEW AND HOW TO PASS IT

During the RAF selection process you will be required to sit a number of interviews depending on the choice of career you make. For some of the more technical or demanding posts you will be required to attend a specialist interview which will be at an RAF base. These can last up to three days depending on the career. This is also an opportunity for you to see what the job is like and meet some of the people you'd be expected to work with once you have passed your initial training.

The first interview however will be held at your local Armed Forces Careers Officer and will be undertaken with a member of the RAF recruitment team. The duration of the interview will very much depend on your responses to the questions. However, you can expect the interview to last for approximately 30 minutes. The questions that you will be assessed against during the initial interview will normally be taken from the following areas:

- The reasons why you want to join the RAF;
- What choice of career you are most interested in, the reason for choosing that career, and the skills you have to match the role;
- What information you already know about the RAF, its lifestyle and training;
- Information relating to your hobbies and interests including sporting/team activities;
- Any personal responsibilities that you currently have at home, in your education or at work;
- Information about your family and your partner and what they think about you joining.
- Information based around your initial application;
- Your experience of work and education;
- Your emotional stability and your maturity;
- Your drive and determination to succeed.
- Having a positive reaction to a disciplined environment and towards people in positions of authority.

Before I move on to a number of sample interview questions and responses I want to explain a little bit about interview technique and how you can come across in a positive manner during the interview. During my career in the Fire Service I sat on many interview panels assessing people who wanted to become firefighter's. As you can imagine there were some good applicants and there were also some poor ones. Let me explain the difference between a good applicant and a poor one.

A GOOD APPLICANT

A good applicant is someone who has taken the time to prepare. They have researched both the organisation they are applying to join and also the role that they are being interviewed for. They may not know every detail about the organisation and the role but it will be clear that they have made an effort to find out important facts and information. They will be well presented at the interview and they will be confident, but not over confident. As soon as they walk into the interview room they will be polite and courteous and they will sit down in the interview chair only when invited to do so. Throughout the interview they will sit up right in the chair and communicate in a positive manner. If they do not know the answer to a question they will say so and they won't try and waffle. At the end of the interview they will ask positive questions about the job or the organisation before shaking hands and leaving.

A POOR APPLICANT

A poor applicant could be any combination of the following. They will be late for the interview or even forget to turn up at all. They will have made little effort to dress smart and they will have carried out little or no preparation. When asked questions about the job or the organisation they will have little or no knowledge. Throughout the interview they will appear to be unenthusiastic about the whole process and will look as if they want the interview to be over as soon as possible. Whilst sat in the interview chair they will slouch and fidget. At the end of the interview they will try to ask clever questions that are intended to impress the panel.

Earlier on in the guide I made reference to a 'mock interview'. I strongly advise that you try out a mock interview before the real thing. You'll be amazed at how much your confidence will improve. All you need to do is get your parents or a friend to sit down with you and ask you the interview questions that are contained within this guide. Try to answer them as if you were at the real interview. The more mock interviews you try the more confident you'll become.

Now let's take a look at a number of sample interview questions. Please note that these questions are not guaranteed to be the exact ones you'll come up against at the real interview but they are great starting point in your preparation. Use the sample responses that I have provided as a basis for your own preparation. Construct your answers on your own opinions and experiences.

SAMPLE INTERVIEW QUESTION NUMBER 1

Why do you want to join the Royal Air Force?

This is an almost guaranteed question during the selection interview so there should be no reason why you can't answer it in a positive manner. Only you will know the real reason why you want to join but consider the following benefits before you construct your response:

- A career in the RAF presents a challenge that is not available in the majority of other jobs or careers;
- A career in the RAF will provide you with professional training and ongoing personal development;
- A career in the RAF will offer you the chance to work in a highly professional organisation that prides itself on high standards;
- The RAF is an organisation that people have a huge amount of respect for. Therefore those people who join it are very proud to be a part of such a team.

Try to display a good level of motivation when answering questions of this nature. The Royal Air Force is looking for people who want to become a professional member of their team and who understand their way of life. It should be your own decision to join the Royal Air Force and you should be attracted to what this career has to offer. If you have been pushed into joining by your family then you shouldn't be there! On the following page I have provided you with a sample response to this question.

SAMPLE RESPONSE TO INTERVIEW QUESTION NUMBER 1

Why do you want to join the Royal Air Force?

'I have wanted to join the Royal Air Force for a couple of years now and I have been working very hard to pass selection. Having studied the RAF recruitment literature and the RAF website I am impressed by the professionalism and standards the service sets itself. I would like a career that is fulfilling, challenging and rewarding and I believe that the RAF would provide all of these. During my research I have spoken to serving members of the RAF and every single one of them has had positive things to say about the service. The fact that I would be improving my education and ending up with a trade is just another example of why I want to join the RAF.

Over the last few years I have become more aware of my own skills and qualities and I believe these would be very well suited to the RAF. I enjoy being away from home and I also like to take responsibility. For example, I was recently made captain of my football team and this involves organising team trips and fixtures. I am also a good team player and I like working with different groups of people who have different experiences in life. There is always something to learn in life and I would love to be a part of a service such as the RAF where I would be continually learning new skills.

I have seriously considered the implications that joining a service such as the RAF would have on both my personal life and social life and I have discussed these with my family and my partner. They have given me their full support and they promise to help me achieve my goal of joining the Royal Air Force. Even though I know the training will be hard I am certain I can pass it with flying colours and if I am successful I promise that I will work very hard to pass every exam.'

SAMPLE INTERVIEW QUESTION NUMBER 2

What does your family think of you wanting to join the Royal Air Force?

What your family think about you wanting to join the RAF is very important, simply for the reason that you will need their support both during your training and during your career. I can remember my parents being fully behind my decision to join the Armed Forces and I'm glad that they were for a very good reason. After about two weeks into my basic training I started to feel a little bit home sick; like any young man would do being away from home for a long period of time. I rang my father and discussed with him how I felt. After about five minutes chat on the phone I felt perfectly fine and I no longer felt homesick. During that conversation he reminded me how hard I had worked to get a place on the course and that he and my mother wanted me to succeed. For that reason alone I was glad that I had the support of my parents.

Before you apply to join the RAF it is important that you discuss your choice of career with either your parents or your guardian. If you have a partner then obviously you will need to discuss this with them too. If they have any concerns whatsoever then I would advise you take them along with you to the Armed Forces Careers Office so they can discuss these concerns with the trained recruitment staff. Get their full support as you may need it at some point during your career, just like I did.

On the following page I have provided a sample response to help you prepare.

SAMPLE RESPONSE TO INTERVIEW QUESTION NUMBER 2

What does your family think of you wanting to join the Royal Air Force?

'Before I made my application I discussed my choice of career with both my parents and my boyfriend. Initially they were apprehensive but they could see how motivated and excited I was as I explained everything I had learnt so far about the service. I showed them the recruitment literature and even took them around an RAF museum to get them on board with my application. I understand that it is important they support me during my application and I now have their full backing. In fact, they are now more excited about the fact I'll be leaving home than I am! I have also told them everything I know about the training I will go through and the conditions I will serve under. They are aware that the Royal Air Force has a brilliant reputation and this has helped them to further understand why I want to join. They are also looking forward to hopefully seeing me at my passing out parade if I am successful and, therefore, I have their full backing.'

SAMPLE INTERVIEW QUESTION NUMBER 3

What grades did you achieve at school and how do you feel about them?

Questions that relate to your education are common during the initial RAF interview. In addition to this question they may also ask you questions that relate to which schools or educational establishments you attended.

This kind of question is designed to assess your attitude to your grades and also how hard you worked whilst at school. As you can imagine, your grades will generally reflect how hard you worked and therefore you will need to be totally honest in your response. If like me, you achieved very few educational qualifications then you will need to explain what you intend to do about it in the future. Despite leaving school with few GCSE's it was later on in my life that I really started to realise my academic potential. Whilst waiting for my start date when I joined the Armed Forces I went back to college and embarked on a foundation course to improve my grades. If you achieve the grades you wanted during education then congratulations, you'll find this question easier to answer.

Take a look at the following sample response which is based on my own personal circumstances at the time of joining.

SAMPLE RESPONSE INTERVIEW QUESTION NUMBER 3

What grades did you achieve at school and how do you feel about them?

'To be totally honest I didn't do as well as I had hoped. The reason for this was that I didn't work hard enough during the build up to the exams. I'd put in some preparation but I now realise I should have worked harder. In order to improve my grades I have decided to embark on a foundation course at my local college and I start this in a month's time. In the build up to selection I have been working hard on my academic abilities and know that I can do well on the written tests. I've certainly learnt from my lack of educational qualifications and I can assure you that if I am successful I will be working extremely hard to pass all of my exams during both my basic training and my branch training.'

SAMPLE INTERVIEW QUESTION NUMBER 4

What responsibilities do you have either at work, school or at home?

When you join the RAF you will automatically become responsible for a number of things. Apart from being responsible for the upkeep of your kit and your equipment you will also have additional responsibilities such as cleaning, ironing and making sure you are on time for every lesson, tutorial and drill. Those people who have had little or no experience whatsoever prior to joining may find this new burden difficult to cope with. Therefore, having already held positions of responsibility prior to applying will work in your favour. If you've never had any responsibility in your life then now is the time to make a change. Start taking responsibility for household tasks such as the washing and cleaning. Learn how to iron your own clothes or take on a part time/full time job that requires you to be responsible for a specific role. You may even decide to join a group or youth organisation such as the air cadets or scouts. Whatever you do, make sure you are responsible for carrying out set tasks and jobs and also make sure you carry out those jobs professionally and to the best of your ability.

Now take a look at the following sample response to this question.

SAMPLE RESPONSE TO INTERVIEW QUESTION NUMBER 4

What responsibilities do you have either at work, school or at home?

'I currently hold a few responsibilities both at home and in my part time job. I'm responsible for cleaning the house top to bottom once a week and I usually do this on a Sunday before I go and play football for my local team. I'm also captain of my football team which means I have to arrange the fixtures, book the football ground and I also collect the kit at the end of the match and get it washed and dried for the following week's fixture.

I have just started a new job at my local supermarket where I'm responsible for serving customers and making sure stock levels are kept up. This involves cross checking current stock levels with required standards and I have to report daily to my manager with any discrepancies or missing items or goods. Whilst serving the customer I'm responsible for ensuring I give them a good level of service and I also have to check people for identification if they appear to be under the required age to purchase alcohol or cigarettes.

I enjoy taking on responsibility as it gives me a sense of achievement. I understand that I will need to be responsible during my RAF training for not only the upkeep of my kit and equipment but I'll also have to make sure I am punctual and that I make the time to study hard in the evening for my exams.'

SAMPLE INTERVIEW QUESTION NUMBER 5

How do you think you will cope with the discipline, regimentation and routine in the RAF?

When you join the RAF you will be joining a military organisation that has set procedures, standards and discipline codes. Procedures, standards and discipline codes are there for a very good reason. They ensure that the organisation operates at its optimum best and without them things would go wrong, and people would either be injured or at worst killed. To some people these important aspects of RAF life will come as a shock when they join. The RAF recruitment staff will want to know that you are fully prepared for this change in lifestyle. They are investing time, effort and resources into your training so they want to know that you can cope with their way of life.

When answering this type of question you need to demonstrate both your awareness of what the RAF life involves and also your positive attitude towards the disciplined environment. Study the recruitment literature and visit the careers website to get a feel for the type of training you will be going through. On the following page we have provided you with a sample response to this question.

SAMPLE RESPONSE TO INTERVIEW QUESTION NUMBER 5

How do you think you will cope with the discipline, regimentation and routine in the RAF?

'I believe I would cope with it very well. In the build up to selection I have been trying to implement routine and discipline into my daily life. I've been getting up at 6am every weekday morning and going on a 3 mile run. This will hopefully prepare me for the early starts that I'll encounter during training. I've also been learning how to iron my own clothes and I've been helping around the house with the cleaning and washing, much to the surprise of my parents!

I fully understand that the RAF needs a disciplined workforce if it is to function as effectively as it does. Without that discipline things could go wrong and if I did not carry out my duties professionally then I could endanger somebody's life. For example, I want to become an Aircraft Technician which is an extremely responsible job. If I did not carry out my job correctly and also look after my tools and equipment then I would not only be failing in my duty, but I would also be endangering other people's lives. I fully understand why discipline is required and believe I would cope with it well. I understand that being in the RAF isn't a 9-5 job but instead you are required to take on tasks whenever required.

I have read all of the RAF recruitment literature and I know there are people from every background working in the team. I know that I can bring something to the team too.'

SAMPLE INTERVIEW QUESTION NUMBER 6

How do you think you will cope with being away from home and losing your personal freedom?

This type of question is one that needs to be answered positively. The most effective way to respond to it is to provide the recruitment staff with examples of where you have already lived away from home for a period of time. This could be either with your school or college, an adventure trip, camping with friends or even with a youth organisation. Try to think of occasions when you have had to fend for yourself or even 'rough it' during camps or adventure trips. If you are already an active person who spends very little time sat at home in front of the television or computer, then you will probably have no problem with losing your personal freedom. During your time in the RAF there'll be very little time to sit around doing nothing anyway. So, if you're used to being active before you join, then this is a plus.

Take a look at the sample response on the following page and try to structure your own response around this.

SAMPLE RESPONSE TO INTERVIEW QUESTION NUMBER 6

How do you think you will cope with being away from home and losing your personal freedom?

'I already have some experience of being away from home so I believe I would cope quite well. Whilst serving with the Air Cadets I was introduced to the RAF way of life and I fully understand what it is like to be away from home. Having said that, I am not complacent and I have been working hard to improve my fitness and academic skills. To be honest with you, I'm not the kind of person who sits around at home watching television or sitting at the computer, so I'm hardly in doors anyway. In terms of losing my personal freedom I'm looking forward to the routine and regimentation that the RAF will provide as I believe this will bring some positive structure to my life. Even though I am young I want to ensure that I have a good future and I believe a career in the RAF will bring me just that, providing that is, I work hard during training.

During my time in the Air Cadets I've been away on a couple of camps and I really enjoyed this. We learnt how to fend for ourselves whilst away and I loved the fact that I was meeting new and interesting people. I understand that RAF training will be difficult and intense but I am fully prepared for this. I am confident that I will cope with the change in lifestyle very well.'

SAMPLE INTERVIEW QUESTION NUMBER 7

Are you involved in any sporting activities and how do you keep yourself fit?

This is an almost guaranteed question during the RAF selection interview so make sure you have something positive to respond with. When answering questions based around your own physical fitness and the types of sporting activities you are involved in you need to be honest, but bear in mind the following points:

Although you don't have to be super fit to join the RAF you do need to have a good level of physical fitness, so being fit in the first instance is obviously an advantage. The RAF prides themselves on their ability to work as an effective team unit. Those people who engage in active team sports are more likely to be competent team members. If you play a team sport then this will be a good thing to tell the interviewers. If you don't, then it might be a good idea to go and join one!

Regardless of the above points, remember that if you don't do any physical activity whatsoever then you will score low in this area. Make sure you partake in some form of physical activity.

On the following page we have provided a sample response to help you prepare.

SAMPLE RESPONSE TO INTERVIEW QUESTION NUMBER 7

Are you involved in any sporting activities and how do you keep yourself fit?

'Yes I am. I currently play in my local netball team and have been doing so for a number of years now. Maintaining a good level of fitness is something I enjoy. In fact, in addition to my netball involvement I also go running 3 times a week. I'm aware that during the initial RAF recruit training course I will be pushed to my limits so I need to be prepared for that. I believe the fact that I play team sports will help me get through my training.

I enjoy playing in the netball team because when we are losing to another team everyone always pulls together and we work hard to try and win the game back. After the game we all meet in the club bar for a drink and chat about the game. At the next training session we always work on our weak areas and try to look for ways to improve as a team. Keeping fit is important to me and something that I want to continue throughout my career if I am successful in joining the RAF. I have also been working hard to pass the pre-joining fitness test and I have made sure that I can easily pass the minimum standard'.

SAMPLE INTERVIEW QUESTION NUMBER 8

What do you think the qualities of a good team player are?

As you are already aware, the RAF prides itself on the ability to operate as an effective team member. Therefore, having knowledge of how a team operates and the qualities required to become a competent team player would be an advantage. You will recall during an earlier section of the guide I made reference to some of the more important qualities that are required to operate as an effective team player. These included:

- An ability to interact and work with others, regardless of their age, sex, religion, sexual orientation, background, disability or appearance;
- Being able to communicate with everyone in the team and provide the appropriate level of support and encouragement;
- Being capable of carrying out tasks correctly, professionally and in accordance with guidelines and regulations;
- Being focused on the team's goal(s);
- Having a flexible attitude and approach to the task;
- Putting the needs of the team first before your own;
- Putting personal differences aside for the sake of the team;
- Being able to listen to others suggestions and contributions;

When responding to this type of question it would be an advantage if you could back up your response with an example of where you already work in a team. Take a look at the following sample response before creating your own based on your own experiences and ideas.

SAMPLE RESPONSE TO INTERVIEW QUESTION NUMBER 8

What do you think the qualities of a good team player are?

'A good team player must have many different qualities including an ability to listen carefully to a given brief. If you don't listen to the brief that is provided then you can't complete the task properly. In addition to listening carefully to the brief you must be able to communicate effectively with everyone in the team. This will include providing support for the other team members and also listening to other people's suggestions on how a task can be achieved. You also have to be able to work with anyone in the team regardless of their age, background, religion, sexual orientation, disability or appearance. You can't discriminate against anyone and if you do, then there is no place for you within that team. A good team player must also be able to carry out his or her job professionally and competently. When I say competently I mean correctly and in accordance with guidelines and training. You should also be focused on the team's goal and not be distracted by any external factors. Putting the needs of the team first is paramount. Finally a good team player must be flexible and be able to adapt to the changing requirements of the team.

I already have some experience of working in a team and I know how important it is to work hard at achieving the task. I have a part time job at weekends working in my local supermarket and every week we have a team briefing. During the team briefings my manager will inform us what jobs need to be carried out as a priority. During one particular meeting he asked three of us to clear a fire escape that had become blocked with cardboard boxes, debris and rubbish. He also asked us to come up with a plan to prevent it from happening again. We quickly set about the task carefully removing the rubbish and I had the responsibility of arranging for a refuse collection company to come and dispose of the rubbish. We also had to work together to find ways of preventing the rubbish from being haphazardly disposed in the same way again in the future. We sat down together and wrote out a memorandum for our manager that he could distribute to all staff. At the end of the job we'd worked well to achieve the task and no more rubbish was ever disposed in the fire escape again. My manager was very pleased with the job we'd done.'

SAMPLE INTERVIEW QUESTION NUMBER 9

What do you do in your spare time?

With questions of this nature the Royal Air Force recruitment staff are looking to see if you use your leisure time wisely. This will tell them a lot about your attitude and motivation. We all know that some people spend their spare time doing nothing, or watching TV and playing computer games. When you join the RAF you won't have much time do nothing, so tell them that you are active and that you are doing worthwhile things. For example, if you are involved in any sports, outdoor activities or are part of any youth organisation such as the Air Cadets, then these are good things to tell them. You may also be involved in voluntary work or charity work and, once again, such pastimes will work in your favour if mentioned at interview. If you currently do very little with your spare time then now is a good time to make a lifestyle change. Embark on a fitness routine or join an activity club or organisation.

On the following page I have provided you with a sample response to this question.

SAMPLE RESPONSE TO INTERVIEW QUESTION NUMBER 9

What do you do in your spare time?

'During my spare time I like to keep active, both physically and mentally. I enjoy visiting the gym three times a week and I have a structured workout that I try and vary every few months to keep my interest up. When I attend the gym I like to work out using light weights and I also enjoy using the indoor rower. I always try and beat my best time over a 2000 metre distance.

I'm also currently doing a weekly evening class in Judo, which is one of my hobbies. I haven't achieved any grades yet but I am taking my first one in a few weeks time. I'm also a member of the local Air Cadet Force, which is an evening's commitment every week and the occasional weekend. Of course, I know when it is time to relax and usually do this by either listening to music or playing snooker with my friends but, overall, I'm quite an active person. I certainly don't like sitting around doing nothing. I understand that if I'm successful in joining the RAF there will be plenty of things to do in the evenings to keep me occupied, such as the free gym and other various social events.'

SAMPLE INTERVIEW QUESTION NUMBER 10

Can you tell me about any achievements you have experienced during your life so far?

Those people who can demonstrate a history of achievement during the RAF interview are far more likely to pass the initial training course. Demonstrating a history of achievement already will work in your favour. Having achieved something in your life demonstrates that you have the ability to see things through to the end, something which is crucial to your career in the RAF. It also shows that you are motivated and determined to succeed.

Try to think of examples where you have succeeded or achieved something relevant in your life. Some good examples of achievements are as follows:

- Winning a trophy with a football or hockey team;
- GCSE's and other educational qualifications;
- Duke of Edinburgh's Awards;
- Being given responsibility at work or at school;
- Raising money for charity.

Obviously you will have your own achievements that you want to add in your response, but on the following page I have provided you with an example.

Once you have read it try to think of occasions in your life where you have achieved something of importance.

SAMPLE RESPONSE TO INTERVIEW QUESTION NUMBER 10

Can you tell me about any achievements you have experienced during your life so far?

'Yes I can. So far in my life I have achieved quite a few things that I am proud of. To begin with I achieved good grades whilst at school including a grade 'A' in English. I worked very hard to achieve my grades and I'm proud of them. At weekends I play rugby for a local team and I've achieved a number of things with them. Apart from winning the league last year we also held a charity match against the local Police rugby team. We managed to raise £500 for a local charity which was great achievement.

More recently I managed to achieve a huge increase in my fitness levels. Because I am applying to join the RAF Regiment I have been working very hard to improve my strength, fitness and overall stamina. I have increased my scores on the bleep test and I can now swim fifty lengths of my local pool. When I started I could hardly mange ten lengths!

I have learnt that you have to work hard in life if you want to achieve things and I have a good positive attitude to hard work. My own personal motto is 'work hard and you'll be rewarded'.

SAMPLE INTERVIEW QUESTION NUMBER 11

What are your strengths and what are you good at?

This is a common interview question that is relatively easy to answer. The problem with it is that many people use the same response. It is quite an easy thing to tell the interviewer that you are dedicated and the right person for the job. However, it is a different thing backing it up with evidence!

If you are asked this type of question make sure you are positive during your response and show that you actually mean what you are saying. Then, back up the strengths you have mentioned with examples of when you have been something that you say you are. For example, if you tell the panel that you are a motivated person, back it up with an example in your life where you have achieved something through sheer motivation and determination.

On the following page I have provided a sample response to this type of question.

SAMPLE RESPONSE TO INTERVIEW QUESTION NUMBER 11

What are your strengths and what are you good at?

'To begin with, I'm a determined person who likes to see things through to the end. For example, I recently ran a marathon for charity. I'd never done this kind of thing before and found it very hard work, but I made sure I completed the task. Another strength of mine is that I'm always looking for ways to improve myself. As an example, I have been preparing for the RAF selection process by performing mock mathematical tests. I noticed that I was getting a number of fraction and decimal questions wrong, so in order to improve I decided to get some personal tuition at my college to ensure that I could pass this part of the test. Finally, I would say that one of my biggest strengths is that I'm a great team player. I really enjoy working in a team environment and achieving things through a collaborative approach. For example, I play in a local rugby team and we recently won the league trophy for the first time since the club was established some 50 years ago.'

SAMPLE INTERVIEW QUESTION NUMBER 12

What are your weaknesses?

Now this is a difficult question to answer. We all have weaknesses and anyone who says they haven't, is probably not telling truth. However, you must be very careful how you respond to this question. Apart from being truthful you must also provide a weakness that you are working hard on to improve. You should also remember that you are joining a disciplined service that requires hard work, determination and a will to succeed. So, if you are the type of person who cannot get up in the morning and you keep making regular mistakes at work or at school, then the RAF might not be for you.

The key to responding to this type of question is to be truthful but to also back it up with examples of what you are doing to improve your weakness. Take a look at the following example.

SAMPLE RESPONSE TO INTERVIEW QUESTION NUMBER 12

What are your weaknesses?

'I have to be honest, whilst studying for the RAF aptitude tests I found that I wasn't particularly good at the sample numerical reasoning questions. Even though I did alright in my Maths GCSE at school, I seemed to be struggling with these questions. Anyway, I didn't let this deter me in my pursuit to joining the RAF so I decided to get some personal tuition at my local college. I managed to find a free evening class that helped me to understand how to carry out the questions. After a couple of week's tuition I soon noticed a big improvement in my scores and my ability to answer these questions. I'm still attending the evening classes which I've found to be a great boost to my confidence. I feel very confident that when I do come to sit the tests I'll be able to achieve the required scores.'

SAMPLE INTERVIEW QUESTION NUMBER 13

Can you tell me what you have learnt about your chosen career?

Once again, an almost guaranteed question, so make sure you prepare for it fully. The only information you will need is either in the recruitment literature that you're provided with, or on the RAF careers website at www.raf.mod.uk. For example, if you want to join the RAF as an Aircraft Technician (Mechanical) then visit the website and read up on the information available regarding this career. I also advise that you learn as much as possible about the training that you'll be required to undertake if you are successful. You should also ask your AFCO recruitment advisor for more information relating to your chosen career and training. They will be able to point you in the right direction.

On the following page I have provided a sample response to this question for somebody who is hoping to join as an Aircraft Technician. Use the example to create your own response, relevant to your own chosen trade. You may even wish to look at other avenues or research to improve your knowledge and further demonstrate your determination to succeed. For example, if you wish to join the RAF as a Photographer then why not buy a book relating to photographers or embark on an evening class and start learning before you even join!

SAMPLE RESPONSE TO INTERVIEW QUESTION NUMBER 13

Can you tell me what you have learnt about your chosen career?

'I'm aware that up to one third of people who are employed by the RAF work in engineering. As an Aircraft Technician it will be my responsibility to maintain the airframes and engines of the RAF's aircraft. This will include the different mechanical components, hydraulics, gear boxes and flying controls to name just a few. It is important to ensure that the aircraft are always ready to fly at all times. Another important part of this job is the preparation of the aircraft before they take off and also checking them for damage when they return from flight. Finally, Aircraft Technicians are responsible for the complete overhaul of the aircraft after set periods of time. I also understand that my job wouldn't be 9 to 5 and I'd be required to work day shifts and night shifts. Being flexible is crucial to the role.

During my training I will start off as an Aircraft Maintenance Mechanic. This role will be vital to my development as I will get to learn from already serving Aircraft Technicians. At this initial stage of my training I will get to help the other members of the team replace aircraft components and also check the aircraft for damage after sorties and missions making sure they are ready to fly again quickly. I'm also aware that the training for this RAF career earns you an Engineering Certificate at Level 3 and Key Skills at Level 2. Once I've completed my training and my NVQ Level 3 I will be awarded with an Advanced Apprenticeship in aeronautical engineering.'

SAMPLE INTERVIEW QUESTION NUMBER 14

What has attracted you to your chosen career?

This type of question is designed to see if there are any genuine reasons why you have chosen your particular career. Some applicants get carried away with the glamour of some of the posts that are available; without putting any serious thought into why they actually want the job. When preparing your response to this question you need to think about the skills you have already gained that are relevant to the role, and also any experiences you have that would assist you in becoming competent at that role. For example, an applicant who has been working as a chef in a local restaurant or pub would have plenty of skills and experiences that are relevant to the role.

Previous experiences and skills are not a pre-requisite for some jobs in the RAF; however, you will need to provide genuine reasons why you have chosen your particular choice of career. Take a look at the following sample response to this question which will assist you during your preparation.

SAMPLE RESPONSE TO INTERVIEW QUESTION NUMBER 14

What has attracted you to your chosen career?

(Response for applicant applying to become a chef)

'I have always had a passion for cooking. Ever since I was young I have had a keen interest in this area and my grades at college will reflect that. After school had finished I embarked on a Professional Chef Diploma which I loved and passed with excellent grades. More recently I have been working part time as a chef at my local Bistro. It make sense to me to chose a job in the RAF that is both relevant to my skills and experiences and also a job that I will never become bored of. I often receive positive feedback from the customers who come to the Bistro, and that makes the hard work and training worthwhile. Because of my experiences as a chef, and the training and qualifications I have already gained, I believe I would be a great asset to the RAF team.'

SAMPLE INTERVIEW QUESTION NUMBER 15

Can you tell me whereabouts in the world the RAF are operating right now?

If you put plenty of work into your preparation then you will undoubtedly get to find out the whereabouts of the RAF around the world. Of course, this will change as the weeks and month's progress but one of the most effective ways to find out where the RAF are operating right now is to visit the Ministry of Defence website at www.mod.uk. From here you will be able to access instant and up to date information relevant to the RAF's current operations. Remember to regularly check the website for updates.

Take a look at the following answer to this question which is only relevant to the RAF's operations at the time of writing.

SAMPLE RESPONSE TO INTERVIEW QUESTION NUMBER 15

Can you tell me whereabouts in the world the RAF are operating right now?

Response correct at time of writing

'At the current time the RAF are deployed at many different locations around the world. Starting at home, the RAF is defending the United Kingdom with both the Tornado F3 and Typhoon F2. These are based at RAF Coningsby which is in Lincolnshire, and also at RAF Leuchars which is located in Fife. The aircraft are strategically placed at these locations so that they can take off at a moments notice. The RAF is also responsible for managing the Wideawake airfield which is located in the Ascension Islands. This airfield acts as a link for the Armed Forces to the Falklands Islands and also to St Helena. There is a small detachment from the 1 Air Mobility Wing Unit from RAF Lyneham based at the airfield and their job is to ensure the smooth running of each flight.

The RAF is also extremely active in the South Atlantic, especially in the Falklands Islands. The RAF operates a number of patrols around this area which act as a deterrent to any potential threats. In addition to these patrols the RAF operates a Search and Rescue facility to the Island and is also involved in fishing patrols and air transport patrols by way of a Hercules aircraft. There is also a Tornado F3 squadron based on the island at Mount Pleasant airfield. This acts as security for the island and the personnel who live there.

The RAF is also based in Cyprus at Aktrotiri. From here the RAF supports operations in Afghanistan. The base itself is used as a forward mounting base for ops in the Middle East. Its secondary role is for Fast Jet Weapons Training. The RAF plays a huge part in United Nations operations at present they have personnel based in South Korea, Africa and also as part of the peace keeping operations in Lebanon.

An example of the RAF's more permanent commitments is the managing of the Gibraltar airport. From here the RAF will look after military and civilian movements into and out of the airport.'

SAMPLE INTERVIEW QUESTION NUMBER 16

What are the different ranks for both non-commissioned and commissioned staff in the RAF?

This question assesses your knowledge of the ranks within the RAF. It is a simple question and one that should be relatively easy to respond to. Having an understanding of the different ranks for both commissioned and non-commissioned staff will be an obvious advantage for when you start your initial training. Basically 'commissioned' staff are Officers within the RAF. The 'commission' is earnt following the successful completion of training and it is received from the Queen. The commission entitles an Officer in the RAF to give orders to other people who are at a lower rank than to themselves.

Here are the ranks within the RAF for you to study:

Non-commissioned staff

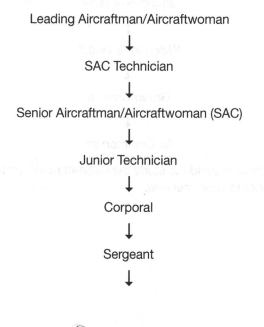

Leading Aircraftman/Aircraftwoman

↓

SAC Technician

↓

Senior Aircraftman/Aircraftwoman (SAC)

↓

Junior Technician

↓

Corporal

↓

Sergeant

↓

Chief Technician

↓

Flight Sergeant

↓

Warrant Officer

Commissioned staff

Pilot Officer

↓

Flying Officer

↓

Flight Lieutenant

↓

Squadron Leader

↓

Wing Commander

↓

Group Captain

↓

Air Commodore

You may also decide to study the different markings for each rank prior to your interview.

SAMPLE INTERVIEW QUESTION NUMBER 17

Name five different RAF bases and their roles?

There are many different RAF bases around the UK and also around the world. Learning all of their names and their roles would be quite a task. However, I believe it is important that you at least know the names, locations and the roles of a number of them. On the RAF website you will be able to find details about each individual airbase and the roles each one carried out.

Take a look at the following sample response to this question.

SAMPLE RESPONSE TO INTERVIEW QUESTION NUMBER 17

Name five different RAF bases and their roles?

'During my research I studied the many different airbases and I even managed to visit a couple of them. The first airbase that I studied is RAF Brize Norton which is based in Caterton, Oxfordshire. This airbase is the largest in the UK and from here the RAF operate air transportation services and air-to-air refuelling operations. In addition to holding large numbers of aircraft such as the VC10 and the TriStar K1 it is also the home of the Parachute Training School. Then there is RAF Gibraltar which is manned by RAF staff. There are no aircraft based there but the airbase is still used by many visiting aircraft. Although I never visited RAF Gibraltar I am aware of its significance as an RAF base. RAF Honnington is located at Bury St Edmunds, Suffolk and this is the RAF Regiment depot. Aircraft have not been at this base since 1993. RAF Uxbridge is based in Middlesex and this is the home of the Number 63 RAF Regiment Squadron and is also the HQ for Music Services. Finally I studied RAF Odiham which is located in Hampshire. Based at RAF Odiham are a number of different Chinook Helicopter Squadrons such as number 7 Squadron, Number 18 Squadron and number 27 Squadron.'

FINAL INTERVIEW TIPS

Within this section of the guide I will provide you with some final tips that will help you prepare for the RAF selection interviews. Remember that your success will very much depend on how prepared you are. Don't forget to work on your interview technique, carry out plenty of research and work on your responses to the interview questions.

- In the build up to the interview carry out plenty of targeted preparation work. Read your recruitment literature and spend time studying the RAF website. Ask the AFCO recruitment advisor to provide you with information about the training you'll undergo for both your chosen career and also your initial training;
- Work on your interview technique and make sure you try out at least one mock interview. This involves getting your family or friends to sit you down and ask you the interview questions that are contained within this guide;
- When you receive your date for the interview make sure you turn up on time. Check your travel and parking arrangements the day before your interview. The last thing you need is to be late for your interview!
- Think carefully about what you are going to wear during the interview. I am not saying that you should go out and buy an expensive suit but I do recommend you make an effort to dress smartly. Having said that, if you do decide to wear a smart suit or formal outfit make sure it is clean and pressed. You can still look scruffy in a suit.
- Personal hygiene is all part and parcel of RAF life. Don't attend the interview unwashed, dirty or fresh from the building site!

- When you walk into the interview room, stand up straight with your shoulders back. Project an image of confidence and be polite, courteous and respectful to the interviewer at all times;
- Don't sit down in the interview chair until invited to do so. This will display good manners;
- Whilst you are in the interview chair sit upright with your hands resting on your knees, palms facing downwards. It is OK to use your hands expressively, but don't overdo it;
- Don't slouch in the chair. At the end of each question readjust your position;
- Whilst responding to the interview questions make sure you speak up and be positive. You will need to demonstrate a level of motivation and enthusiasm during the interview;
- Go the extra mile and learn a little bit about the RAF's history. When the panel ask you "What can you tell us about the Royal Air Force?" you will be able to demonstrate that you have made an effort to look into their history as well as their modern day activities;
- Ask positive questions at the end of the interview. Don't ask questions such as "How much leave will I get?" or "How often do I get paid?"
- If you are unsure about a question try not to 'waffle'. If you do not know the answer, then it is OK to say so. Move on to the next question and put it behind you.
- Finally, believe in yourself and be confident.

CHAPTER SEVEN

HOW TO GET RAF FIT

FREE BONUS SECTION

INTRODUCTION

Welcome to your FREE 'How to get RAF Fit' information guide. Within this guide I have provided you with a number of exercises and tips that will assist you during your preparation for the Pre-Joining Fitness Test (PJFT). At the time of writing the PJFT consists of a 1.5 mile run in a time of 12 minutes and 12 seconds for men and 14 minutes and 35 seconds for women. The test will be carried out at either your local Armed Forces Careers Office or alternatively a gymnasium. The PJFT for joining the RAF Regiment however is tougher. For the RAF Regiment you will be required to undertake the Multi Stage Fitness Test, sit ups and press ups, a 3 mile run and a swimming test. The test is undertaken over three days at RAF Honnington in Suffolk.

Your preparation for passing the RAF selection process should also include a structured fitness training programme. Do not make the mistake of solely working on your academic ability. If I was going through RAF selection right now then I would mix up my academic studies and my knowledge of the RAF study with a proper structured fitness training programme. For example, if I had scheduled in 60 minutes AST preparation on a particular weekday evening, then I would most probably go for a 3 mile run immediately after my AST work. This would allow me to free my mind from the high concentration levels I would have endured during my study. It would also act as a good way to maintain my concentration levels. In addition to improving your physical fitness levels I also advise that you keep an eye on your diet and try to eat healthy foods whilst drinking plenty of water. This will all go a long way to helping you improve your general well-being and concentration levels.

As with any form of exercise you should consult your doctor first.

WARNING – Ensure you take advice from a competent fitness trainer in relation to the correct execution of any of the exercises contained within this guide. You may find that the technique for carrying out the exercises contained within this guide differs from the requirements of the RAF.

PLANNING YOUR WORKOUTS AND PREPARING FOR THE PRE JOINING FITNESS TEST

The key to a successful fitness preparation strategy is variety and continuous improvement. When you commence your fitness programme you should be highly motivated. The hard part will come a couple of weeks into your fitness programme when your rate of improvement decreases. It is at this point that you must vary your exercise routine in order to ensure that you stay on the right track and so that you don't lose interest. The reason why most people give up on their fitness regime is mainly due to a lack of proper preparation. You will recall that throughout the duration of this guide the word preparation has been integral, and the same word applies when preparing for the fitness tests. Preparation is key to your success and it is essential that you plan your workouts effectively.

Members of the Armed Forces are required to maintain high fitness levels. However, some branches of the Armed Forces require a higher standard than others and your fitness training programme should reflect this. For example, a candidate who is applying to join the Royal Marines or the Parachute Regiment would concentrate a lot more effort on their fitness preparation than say somebody who was applying to join the RAF. Work hard to pass the PJFT but do not spend hours and hours down the gym or out running.

Read on for some great ways to not only pass the Pre-Joining Fitness Test, but to also stay RAF fit all year round.

GET AN ASSESSMENT BEFORE YOU START TRAINING

The first step is to conduct a 'self fitness test'. This should involve the following three areas:

1. A 1.5 mile run in the fastest time possible.
2. As many sit ups as possible in two minutes.
3. As many press ups as possible in two minutes.

The tests will be very easy to perform and you will not need to attend a gym in order to carry them out. However, the 1.5 mile run that forms part of the PJFT is usually carried out on a treadmill. Running on a treadmill requires a different technique than running on the road. Whilst not essential, I would recommend you try running on a treadmill prior to the actual PJFT so that you can become familiar with the technique required.

Once you have done all three tests you should write down your results and keep them safe somewhere. After two weeks of following your new fitness regime, do all three tests again and check your results against the previous week's results. This is a great way to monitor your performance and progress and it will also keep you motivated and focused on your goals.

KEEP A CHECK ON WHAT YOU EAT AND DRINK

Before we get started with stretching and targeted exercises I would also recommend that you write down everything you eat and drink for a whole week. You must include tea, water, milk, biscuits and anything and everything that you digest. You will soon begin to realise how much you are eating and you will notice areas in which you can make some changes. For example, if you are taking sugar with your tea then why not try reducing it or giving it up all together. If you do then you will soon notice the difference. Because you are about to embark on a fitness training routine you will need to fill your body with the right type of fuel. This includes both food and drink. Let's get one thing straight from the offset, if you fill your body with rubbish then your fitness performance is likely to be on a par with rubbish. Fill it with the right nutrients and vitamins then you will perform far more effectively. When I was 26 years old I decided to do my own version of the ironman challenge for a local charity. I swam two miles, then I ran a marathon, before finally completing a 120 mile cycle ride, all one after the other! I managed to raise over £10,000 for a children's hospice in Kent. In the six months prior to the challenge I trained very hard, but I also put just as much effort into what I ate and drank. This would prove crucial to my success in achieving the challenge.

During your fitness training programme I would recommend you totally avoid the high calorie foods that lack the right level of nutrients such as chips, burgers, chocolates, sweets, fizzy drinks and alcohol etc. Instead, replace them with fruit, vegetables, pasta, rice, chicken and fish. You also need to make sure you drink plenty of water throughout the day in order to keep yourself fully hydrated. This will help to keep your concentration levels up which you will need for the AST. Many people who keep fit will use vitamin supplements and energy enhancing drinks. It is my opinion that you don't need any of these providing you drink plenty of water and you stick to a balanced diet that includes the right vitamins and nutrients. Spend your hard earned money on something else instead rather than buying supplements, powders and energy drinks. It is important that you start to look for opportunities to improve your fitness and well-being right from the offset. These areas are what I call 'easy wins'.

YOU DON'T NEED TO LIFT HEAVY WEIGHTS IN ORDER TO PASS THE PJFT

When I applied to join the Fire Service the physical tests were rigorous, demanding and extremely difficult to pass. As part of the assessment I was required to bench press 50kg, 20 times within 60 seconds. It is my strong belief that you do not need to lift heavy weights in order to pass the PJFT. In fact I would go as far to say that you don't need to lift any weights at all, other than your own body weight during press ups. If you do decide to lift weights then you will be better off including some form of light weight work which is specifically targeted at increasing stamina, strength and endurance. Instead of performing bench presses down the gym, replace them with press ups. Instead of performing heavy lateral pull down exercises replace them with pull ups which only utilise your own body weight.

There are some more great exercises contained within this guide and most of them can be carried out without the need to attend a gym.

ONE STEP AT A TIME

Only you will know how fit you are. I advise that you first of all write down the areas that you believe or feel you need to improve on. For example, if after carrying out your three self fitness tests you realise that you are going to struggle to pass the PJFT then embark on a structured running programme that is designed to gradually improve your performance. If you are applying to join the RAF Regiment then make sure you work on your swimming in addition to running, press ups and sit ups.

The key to making improvements is to do it gradually, and at one step at a time. Try to set yourself small goals. When you carry out your initial 'self fitness test' you may find that you can only achieve a few press ups and sit ups. Instead of focusing on a higher target of 50 press ups within 2 minutes, break down your goals into easy to achieve stepping stones. For example, by the end of the first week aim to an additional 10 press ups and sit ups. Then, add another 10 to the second weeks target and so on and so forth. One of the biggest problems that many people encounter when starting a fitness regime is they become bored very quickly.

This then leads to a lack of motivation and desire, and soon the fitness programme stops. Change your exercise routine often in order to maintain your interest levels. Instead of running everyday, try swimming or indoor rowing. This will keep your interest and motivational levels high and it will also work other muscle groups that running cannot touch.

STRETCHING

How many people stretch before carrying out any form of exercise? Very few people is the correct answer. Not only is it irresponsible but it is also placing yourself at high risk from injury. The last thing you need is an injury prior to PJFT, especially after the amount of hard work you will be putting in to ensure you pass. Before I commence with the exercises we will take a look at a few warm up stretches. Make sure you stretch fully before carrying out any exercises. You want your RAF career to be a long one and that means looking after yourself, including stretching! It is also very important to check with your GP that you are medically fit to carry out any form of physical exercise.

The warm-up calf stretch

To perform this stretch effectively you should first of all start off by facing a wall whilst standing upright. Your right foot should be close to the wall and your right knee bent. Now place your hands flat against the wall and at a height that is level with your shoulders. Stretch your left leg far out behind you without lifting your toes and heel off the floor, and lean towards the wall.

Once you have performed this stretch for 25 seconds switch legs and carry out the same procedure for the left leg. As with all exercises contained within this guide, stop if you feel any pain or discomfort.

Stretching the shoulder muscles

To begin with, stand with your feet slightly apart and with your knees only slightly bent. Now hold your arms right out in front of you and with your palms facing away from you with your fingers pointing skywards. Now place your right palm on the back of your left hand and use it to push the left hand further away from you. If you are performing this exercise correctly then you will feel the muscles in your shoulder stretching. Hold for 10 seconds before switching sides.

Stretching the quad muscles (front of the thigh)

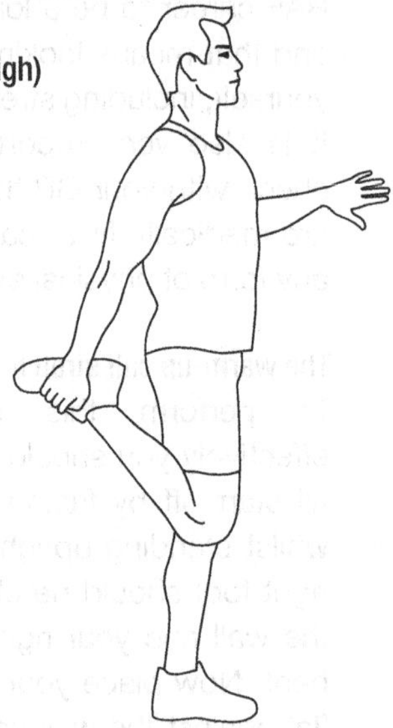

Before you carry out any form of running then it is imperative that you stretch your leg muscles. As you are already aware, as part of the PJFT you are required to run a set distance in a set period of time. It is very important that you stretch fully before the test and your instructor should take you through a number of stretching exercises before you jump on the treadmill.

To begin with, stand with your left hand pressed against the back of a wall or firm surface. Bend your left knee slightly and bring your right heel up to your bottom whilst grasping your foot with your right hand. Your back should be straight and your shoulders, hips and knees should all be in line at all times during the exercise. Hold for 25 seconds before switching legs.

Stretching the hamstring muscles (back of the thigh)

It is very easy to injure your hamstring muscles as a as an Airman/Airwoman, especially with all of the running you'll be doing during your initial basic training. Therefore you must get into the routine of stretching out the hamstring muscles before every training session.

To perform this exercise correctly, stand up straight and place your right foot onto a table or other firm surface so that your leg is almost parallel to the floor. Keep your left leg straight and your foot at a right angle to your leg. Start to slowly move your hands down your right leg towards your ankle until you feel tension on the underside of your thigh. When you feel this tension you know that you are starting to stretch the hamstring muscles. Hold for 25 seconds before switching legs.

I have only covered a small number of stretching exercises within this section; however, it is crucial that you stretch out fully in all areas before carrying out any of the following exercises. Remember to obtain professional advice before carrying out type of exercise.

RUNNING

One of the great ways to prepare for the Pre-Joining Fitness Test is to embark on a structured running programme. You do not need to run extreme long distances in order to gain massively from this type of exercise. As part of the PJFT you will be required to run 1.5 miles in a set period of time. For the RAF Regiment then you will need to do this in a faster time. Don't settle for the minimum standard but instead keep pushing yourself and improving your stamina/fitness levels.

Towards the end of this section I have provided you with a number of weekly training programmes for you to follow. These incorporate running and series of combined exercises that will help you to prepare for the PJFT.

Tips for running

- As with any exercise you should consult a doctor before taking part to make sure that you are medically fit.
- It is certainly worth investing in a pair of comfortable running shoes that serve the purpose for your intended training programme. Your local sports shop will be able to advise you on the types that are best for you. You don't have to spend a fortune to buy a good pair of running shoes.
- It is a good idea to invest in a 'high visibility' jacket or coat so that you can be seen by fast moving traffic if you intend to run on or near the road.
- Make sure you carry out at least 5 whole minutes of stretching exercises not only before but also after your running programme. This can help to prevent injury.
- Whilst you shouldn't run on a full stomach, it is also not good to run on an empty one either. A great food to eat approximately 30 minutes before a run is a banana. This is great for giving you energy.
- Drink plenty of water throughout the day. Drink at least 1.5 litres each day in total. This will keep you hydrated and help to prevent muscle cramp.

- Don't overdo it. If you feel any pain or discomfort then stop and seek medical advice.
- When preparing for the RAF selection process, use your exercise time as a break from your studies. For example, if you have been practising AST tests for an hour why not take a break and go running? When you return from your run you can then concentrate on your studies feeling refreshed

EXERCISES THAT WILL IMPROVE YOUR OVERAL STAMINA AND FITNESS LEVELS

Press-ups

Whilst running is a great way to improve your overall fitness, you will also need to carry out exercises that are designed to improve your upper body strength. These exercises will help you to prepare for the RAF's basic training course.

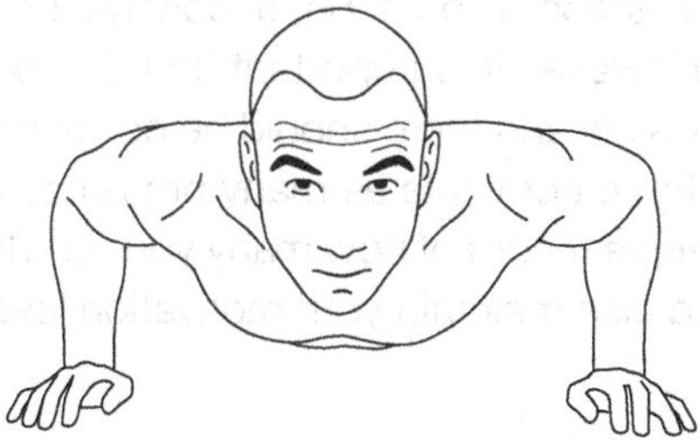

The great thing about press-ups is that you don't have to attend a gym to perform them. However, you must ensure that you can do them correctly as injury can occur. You only need to spend just 5 minutes every day on press-ups, possibly after you go running or even before if you prefer. If you are not used to doing press-ups then start slowly and aim to carry out at least 10.

Even if you struggle to do just 10, you will soon find that after a few days practice at these you will be up to 20+.

Step 1
To begin with, lie on a mat or even surface. Your hands should be shoulder width apart & fully extend the arms.

Step 2
Gradually lower your body until the elbows reach 90°. Do not rush the movement as you may cause injury.

Step 3
Once your elbows reach 90° slowly return to the starting position with your arms fully extended.

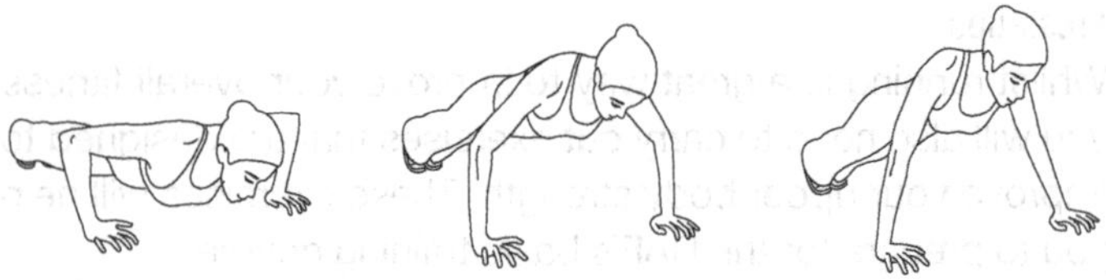

The press up action should be a continuous movement with no rest. However, it is important that the exercise is as smooth as possible and there should be no jolting or sudden movements. Try to complete as many press ups as possible and always keep a record of how many you do. This will keep your focus and also maintain your motivation levels.

Sit-ups
Sit ups are great for building the core stomach muscles. Strong abdominal muscles are important for lifting items of equipment, something which is integral to the role of an Airman/Airwoman. If you are applying to join the RAF Regiment then you will need to have very good all round stamina and strength and sit ups will help you to achieve this.

At the commencement of the exercise lie flat on your back

with your knees bent at a 45° angle and with your feet together. Your hands can either be crossed on your chest, by your sides, or cupped behind your ears as indicated in the diagram below.

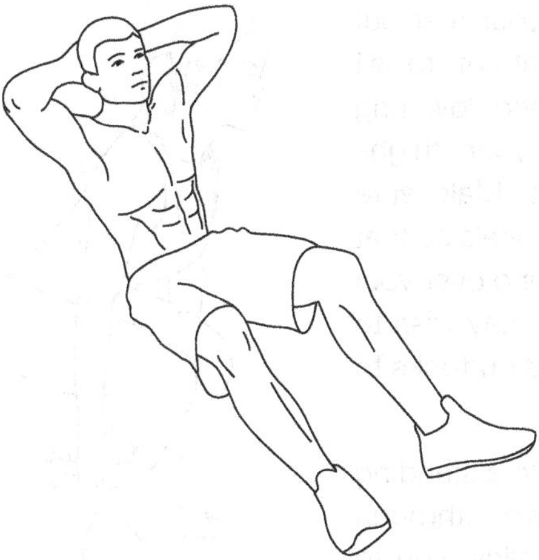

Without moving your lower body, curl your upper torso upwards and in towards your knees, until your shoulder blades are as high off the ground as possible. As you reach the highest point, tighten your abdominals muscles for a brief second. This will allow you to get the most out of the exercise. Now slowly start to lower yourself back to the starting position. You should be aiming to work up to at least 50 effective sit-ups within a two minute period. You will be amazed at how quickly this can be achieved and you will begin to notice your stomach muscles developing.

Squats (these work the legs and bottom)
Squats are a great exercise for working the leg muscles. They are the perfect exercise in your preparation for PJFT as they will develop the leg muscles used for running.

At the commencement of the exercise, stand up straight with your arms at your sides. Concentrate on keeping your feet shoulder-width apart and your head up. Do not look downwards at any point during the exercise. You will see from the diagram below that the person has their lower back slightly arched. They are also holding light weights which can add to the intensity of the exercise.

Now start to very slowly bend your knees while pushing your rear out as though you are about to sit down on a chair. Keep lowering yourself down until your thighs reach pas the 90° point. Make sure your weight is on your heels so that your knees do not extend over your toes. At this point you may wish to tighten your thighs and buttocks to intensify the exercise.

As you come back up to a standing position, push down through your heels which will allow you to maintain your balance. Repeat the exercise 15 to 20 times.

Lunges (these work the thighs and bottom)

You will have noticed throughout this section of the guide that I have been providing you with simple, yet highly effective exercises that can be carried out at home. The lunge exercise is another great addition to the range of exercises that require no attendance at the gym, and they also fit perfectly into the role of an RAF Airman/Airwoman. Simply because they concentrate on building the necessary core muscles to perform the demanding tasks of the job such as bending down and picking up items of equipment.

To begin with, stand with your back straight and your feet together (you may hold light hand weights if you wish to add some intensity to the exercise).

Next, take a big step forward as illustrated in the above diagram making sure you inhale as go and landing with the heel first. Bend the front knee no more than 90 degrees so as to avoid injury. Keep your back straight and lower the back knee as close to the floor as possible. Your front knee should be lined up over your ankle and your back thigh should be in line with your back.

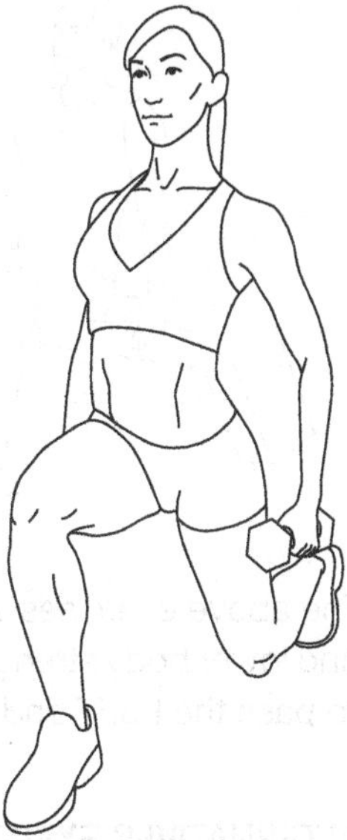

To complete the exercise, exhale and push down against your front heel, squeezing your buttocks tight as you rise back to a starting position.

Try to repeat the exercise 15 to 20 times before switching sides.

Tricep dips

Tricep dips are brilliant at building the muscles at the rear of the arm. Because the tricep muscle is a core part of upper body strength you should spend time developing it. Once again you do not have to attend a gym to work on it.

Step 1
Place your hands shoulder width apart on a bench or immovable object as per the above diagram.

Step 2
Lower your body until your elbows are at an angle of 90 degrees.

Step 3
Push back up so the body returns to the starting position, breathing out on the way up. Ensure that your back remains

close to the bench or immovable object throughout the movement.

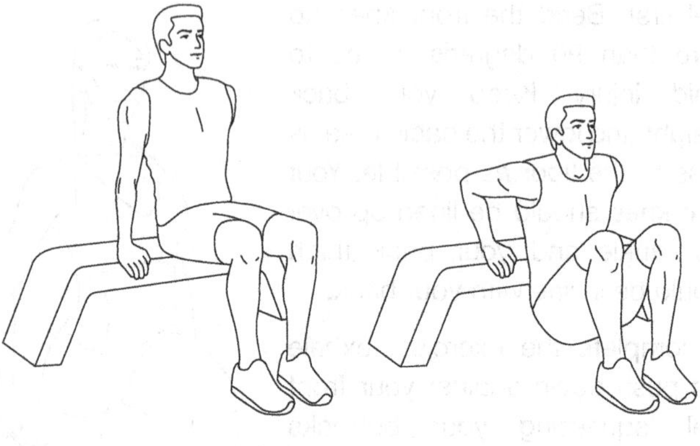

The above exercises will allow you to improve on your upper and lower body strength which will in turn improve your ability to pass the PJFT and the initial RAF basic training course.

ALTERNATIVES EXERCISES

Swimming

Apart from press-ups, lateral raises and the other exercises I have provided you with, another fantastic way to improve your upper body and overall fitness is to go swimming. If you have access to a swimming pool, and you can swim, then this is a brilliant way to improve your fitness and especially your upper body strength. If you are applying to join the RAF Regiment then you will need to be able to swim competently.

If you are not a great swimmer you can start off with short distances and gradually build up your swimming strength and stamina. Breaststroke is sufficient for building good upper body strength providing you put the effort into swimming an effective number of lengths. You may wish to alternate your running programme with the odd day of swimming. If you can swim 10 lengths of a 25-metre pool initially then this is a good base to start from. You will soon find that you can increase this number easily providing that you carry on swimming every week. Try running to your local swimming pool if it is not too far away, swimming 20 lengths of breaststroke, and then running back home.

This is a great way to combine your fitness activity and prevent yourself from becoming bored of your training programme.

The multi stage fitness test or bleep test

A great way to build endurance and stamina is by training with the Multi Stage fitness test or bleep test as it is otherwise called. Once again, if you are applying to join the RAF Regiment then the bleep test forms part of the fitness assessment.

The multi stage fitness test is used by sports coaches and trainers to estimate an athlete's VO2 Max (maximum oxygen uptake). The test is especially useful for players of sports like football, hockey or rugby. You will most certainly have to carry out the test during your initial RAF basic training.

The test itself can be obtained through various websites on the internet and it is great for building your endurance and stamina levels.

TRAINING PROGRAMMES

I believe it is important to add some form of 'structure' to your training programme. Apart from keeping you focused and motivated it will also allow you to measure your results. If I was going through selection right now then I would get myself a small notebook and pencil and keep a check of my times, distances, repetitions and exercises. I would try to improve in each area as each week passes. In order to help you add some form of structure to your training regime I have provided you with four sample training programmes of differing intensity. Before you carry out any form of exercise make sure you consult your doctor to ensure you are fit and healthy. Start off slowly and gradually increase the pace and intensity of your exercises.

You will notice that each of the exercises provided as part of the training programmes is specifically designed to increase your ability during the PJFT and the basic training course.

Training programme 1

Day 1	Day 2	Day 3	Day 4	Day 5
1.5 mile run (best effort) Record and keep results	3 mile run	Swimming (500 metres) or indoor rowing for 2000 metres	3 mile run	Swimming (500 metres) or indoor rowing for 2000 metres
50 sit ups and 50 press ups or as many as possible	50 sit ups and 50 press ups or as many as possible	10 mile cycle ride	50 sit ups and 50 press ups or as many as possible	50 sit ups and 50 press ups or as many as possible
50 sit ups and 50 press ups or as many as possible	50 sit ups and 50 press ups or as many as possible	10 mile cycle ride	50 sit ups and 50 press ups or as many as possible	50 sit ups and 50 press ups or as many as possible

Days 6 and 7 = Rest days

Training programme 2

Day 1	Day 2	Day 3	Day 4	Day 5
1.5 mile run (best effort) Record and keep results	Swimming (500 metres) or indoor rowing for 3000 metres	5 mile run	2 mile walk at a brisk pace followed by a 3 mile run	Swimming (1000 metres) or indoor rowing for 3000 metres
50 sit ups and 50 press ups or as many as possible	10 mile cycle ride	50 sit ups and 50 press ups or as many as possible		50 sit ups and 50 press ups or as many as possible
30 × Squat thrusts	20 × lunges each side and 30 × Star Jumps	Pull ups (as many as possible)	Pull ups (as many as possible)	30 × Squat thrusts 20 × lunges each side and 30 × Star Jumps

Days 6 and 7 = Rest days

Training programme 3

Day 1	Day 2	Day 3	Day 4	Day 5
1.5 mile run (best effort) Record and keep results	5 mile run	20 mile cycle ride	5 mile run	Swimming (1000 metres)
50 sit ups and 50 press ups or as many as possible	50 sit ups and 50 press ups or as many as possible	3 mile walk at a brisk pace	50 sit ups and 50 press ups or as many as possible	50 sit ups and 50 press ups or as many as possible
Swimming (500 metres)		30 × Squat thrusts 20 × lunges each side and 30 × Star Jumps		30 × Squat thrusts 20 × lunges each side and 30 × Star Jumps

Days 6 and 7 = Rest days

Training programme 4

Day 1	Day 2	Day 3	Day 4	Day 5
1.5 mile run (best effort) Record and keep results	Bleep test (best effort)	7 mile run	Swimming (1000 metres)	10 mile run
50 sit ups and 50 press ups or as many as possible	Pull ups (as many as possible) followed by 50 × Squat thrusts 25 × lunges each side and 50 × Star Jumps	70 sit ups and 70 press ups or as many as possible	Pull ups (as many as possible) followed by 50 × Squat thrusts 25 × lunges each side and 50 × Star Jumps	70 sit ups and70 press ups or as many as possible
Swimming (1000 metres) Followed by a 3 mile brisk walk	20 mile cycle ride	30 × Squat thrusts 20 × lunges each side and 30 × Star Jumps	10 mile cycle ride	Swimming (500 metres) Followed by a 3 mile brisk walk

Days 6 and 7 = Rest days

TIPS FOR STAYING WITH YOUR WORKOUT

The hardest part of your training programme will be sticking with it. In this final section of your fitness guide I will provide some useful golden rules that will enable you to maintain your motivational levels in the build up to the RAF Pre-Joining Fitness Test. In order to stay with your workout for longer, try following these simple rules:

Golden rule number one – Work out often

Aim to train five times each and every week.

Each training session should last between 20 minutes to a maximum of an hour. The quality of training is important so don't go for heavy weights but instead go for a lighter weight with a better technique. On days when you are feeling energetic, take advantage of this opportunity and do more!

Within this guide I have deliberately provided you with a number of 'simple to perform' exercises that are targeted at the core muscle groups required to pass the PJFT and also to prepare you for your RAF initial basic training course. In between your study sessions try carrying out these exercises at home or get yourself out on road running or cycling. Use your study 'down time' effectively and wisely.

Golden rule number two – Mix up your exercises

Your exercise programme should include some elements of cardiovascular (running, bleep test, brisk walking, swimming and cycling), resistance training (weights or own body exercises such as press-ups and sit ups) and, finally, flexibility (stretching). Make sure that you always warm up and warm down.

If you are a member of a gym then consider taking up a class such as Pilates. This type of exercise class will teach you how to build core training into your exercise principles, and show you how to hit your abdominals in ways that are not possible with conventional sit-ups. If you are a member of a gym then a fantastic 'all round' exercise that I strongly recommend is rowing. Rowing will hit every major muscle group in your body and it is also perfect for improving your stamina levels and cardiovascular fitness.

Golden rule number three – Eat a healthy and balanced diet

It is vitally important that you eat the right fuel to give you the energy to train to your full potential. Don't fill your body with rubbish and then expect to train well. Think about what you are eating and drinking, including the quantities, and keep a record of what you are digesting. You will become stronger and fitter more quickly if you eat little amounts of nutritious foods at short intervals.

Golden rule number four – Get help

Try working with a personal trainer or someone else who is preparing for selection. They will ensure that you work hard and will help you to achieve your goals. The mere fact that they are there at your side will add an element of competition to your training sessions! A consultation with a professional nutritionist will also help you improve your eating habits and establish your individual food needs.

Golden rule number five – Fitness is for life

Working out and eating correctly are not short-term projects. They are things that should be as natural to us as brushing our teeth. Make fitness a permanent part of your life by following these tips, and you'll lead a better and more fulfilling life!

Good luck and work hard to improve your weak areas.

A FEW FINAL WORDS

You have now reached the end of the guide and no doubt you will be ready to start preparing for the RAF selection process. Just before you go off and start on your preparation, consider the following.

The majority of candidates who pass the RAF selection process have a number of common factors. These are as follows:

1. They believe in themselves.
The first factor is self-belief. Regardless of what anyone tells you, you can pass the selection process and you can achieve high scores. Just like any job of this nature, you have to be prepared to work hard in order to be successful. You will notice that the AST is a lot harder than the entrance tests for the Army or the Royal Navy and therefore you will need to work hard to pass it. Make sure you have the self-belief to pass the selection process and fill your mind with positive thoughts.

2. They prepare fully.

The second factor is preparation. Those people who achieve in life prepare fully for every eventuality and that is what you must do when you apply to become an Airman/Airwoman with the RAF. Work very hard and especially concentrate on your weak areas. Within this guide I have spoken a lot about preparation. Identify the areas that you are weak on and go all out to improve them.

3. They persevere.

Perseverance is a fantastic word. Everybody comes across obstacles or setbacks in their life, but it is what you do about those setbacks that is important. If you fail at something, then ask yourself 'why' have I failed? This will allow you to improve for next time and if you keep improving and trying, success will eventually follow. Apply this same method of thinking when you apply to join the RAF.

4. They are self-motivated.

How much do you want to join the RAF? Do you want it, or do you really want it? When you apply to join the RAF you should want it more than anything in the world. Your levels of self motivation will shine through when you walk into the AFCO and when you attend the interview. For the weeks and months leading up to the selection process, be motivated as best you can and always keep your fitness levels up as this will serve to increase your levels of motivation.

Work hard, stay focused and be what you want…

Richard McMunn